1999

Mercer Guide to Social Security and Medicare

Authors

J. Robert Treanor, B.A., CEBS
Manager, Social Security Division
William M. Mercer, Incorporated

Dale R. Detlefs, B.A., B.S.C., M.B.A., J.D.
Attorney-at-Law
Former Manager, Social Security Division
William M. Mercer, Incorporated

Robert J. Myers, B.S., M.S., LL.D., F.S.A.
Consulting Actuary
Former Chief Actuary and Deputy Commissioner,
Social Security Administration

Acknowledgment

For assistance in the preparation of this book, grateful acknowledgment is made to Donna A. Clements.

This book is revised annually.

625 billion in benefits in ... one of the 45 million ... ou probably **are** one of the 100 million working ... ecurity who can expect to receive benefits later.

Social Security is not just for retirement. Less than half of that $625 billion for Social Security and Medicare will be paid in monthly benefits to retired workers. The rest will be paid to disabled workers; to the families of workers who have retired, become disabled, or died; and for medical expenses.

You and your employer pay for most of those benefits now. The self-employed pay both halves of the tax.

Social Security taxes have increased, but so have benefits. The maximum retirement benefit at age 65 has more than doubled since 1982.

Social Security is the most important financial protection plan in the country. Any time that your income is affected by the significant events of retirement, severe disability, or death, Social Security could pay substantial benefits that increase with the cost of living.

2

This book explains in simple, practical terms what you need to know about Social Security and Medicare:

- what they **cost** you and your employer,
- what **types of benefits** they provide,
- **how much** you get,
- **when** you get it, and
- how to **make sure** you get it.

Social Security. You're paying for it today. It could be your main source of income tomorrow, if you know what to do and when to do it. Don't miss out. Read this book.

You can't afford **not** to!

Recent Changes

New rules for 1999 result from automatic changes that occur annually and those based on past legislation. Only significant changes that might affect you or your family are explained here. Most are discussed in more detail in the text of this book on the pages indicated.

■ The **maximum earnings on which you pay Social Security taxes** increases from $68,400 to **$72,600.** There is no limit on the earnings upon which you pay the Medicare tax (pages 14 and 16).

■ The **cost-of-living increase in benefits** for December 1998, payable in January 1999, is **1.3%** (page 152).

■ The **earnings limitation** for beneficiaries **under age 65** increases from $9,120 to **$9,600**; for beneficiaries at **ages 65-69,** it increases from $14,500 to **$15,500** (page 54).

■ If you reach 65 in 1998 or 1999, the **delayed retirement credit** is 5½% for each full year that you do not receive your benefits (page 49).

■ **Disability benefits** are not payable to persons disabled solely due to drug addiction or alcoholism.

■ All beneficiaries are strongly encouraged to have their benefits paid by **direct deposit.**

■ The **Medicare Part A deductible** increases from $764 to **$768.** After 60 days in a hospital, you must pay $192 per day for 30 days, and then $384 per day for up to 60 "lifetime reserve" days (page 110).

- The **Medicare Part B monthly premium** increases from $43.80 to **$45.50** (page 113).
- New **Medicare+Choice** options are established (page 138).

Changes in 1999 benefit levels have the following results:

- The 1999 **maximum monthly benefit** for an **age 65** retiree is **$1,373** (compared to $1,342 in 1998).
- **Average monthly benefits** are:
  - ➪ Retired workers $780
  - ➪ Retired couples $1,310
  - ➪ Disabled workers $733
  - ➪ Young widow and two eligible children $1,544
  - ➪ Aged widow (no children) $749

How To Use This Book

We've tried to make it easy. You can read through the whole book and get a clear overview of Social Security and Medicare, or you can turn to a specific section to get the answer to your question. Here's where to find the information you want:

What You Want To Know	Where To Find It
If you want to know about a specific **topic:**	Use the Table of Contents (pages 8-9). It lists each topic under every chapter.

If you can't find an answer to your question, call the Social Security Administration at **800-772-1213.** They are available to help. Social Security and Medicare **are** complicated subjects, but they are also important to you. It's worth a little of your time to learn something about them. Share this book with your family; then keep it handy as an important reference to SOCIAL SECURITY and MEDICARE.

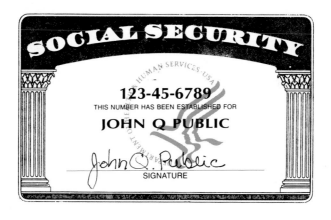

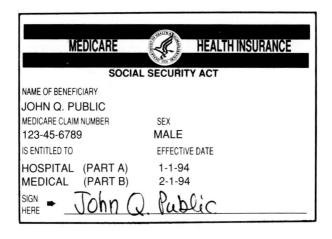

Contents

1 *Who Is Covered*

Almost everyone who works is covered by Social Security and Medicare. Major **exceptions** are:

- **Most federal government employees hired before 1984.** They are covered by Medicare, but usually not by Social Security. Instead, they are covered by the Civil Service Retirement System or a similar pension plan. Beginning in 1957, U.S. military personnel have been under Social Security.

- **About 25% of state and local government employees.** Each state and local government unit with a pension plan decides for itself whether to elect Social Security and Medicare (or Medicare only) coverage; most have joined. Once elected, participation cannot be discontinued. After July 1, 1991, all state and local government employees who are not covered by a retirement plan of their employer are covered by Social Security and Medicare. All state and local government employees hired after March 1986 pay the 1.45% Medicare tax even if they do not have to pay the 6.2% Social Security tax.

- **Railroad workers** are covered under the federal Railroad Retirement system. Workers with coverage under both Railroad Retirement and Social Security have their benefits coordinated.

2 *Who Receives Benefits*

Social Security pays benefits when you retire, become disabled, or die, if eligibility requirements are met.

Your spouse and children may also be eligible for benefits when you become entitled. The following information shows who most often receives Social Security cash benefits. Qualifications are different for each kind of benefit, as described later.

Monthly payments are increased each January to reflect changes in the cost of living.

When You Receive Social Security Benefits

Benefits normally arrive in the month after the month for which the benefit is paid. For example, you receive the benefit for January in February. Since 1997, not all beneficiaries are paid on the same day of the month. Social Security will notify you as to which day of the month you are to be paid.

Social Security strongly encourages all beneficiaries to have their benefits directly deposited in their account with a financial institution.

When You Retire Benefits May Be Paid To:

You
Age 62 or over

Your Spouse
Age 62 or over

Any age, if caring for your child who is under 16 or who is disabled before age 22

Your Unmarried Child
Under 18, or 18 if in high school, or any age if disabled before age 22

When You Become Disabled Benefits May Be Paid To:

You
Any age before Full Retirement Age (page 44)

Your Spouse
Any age, if caring for your child who is under 16 or who is disabled before age 22

Age 62 or over

Your Unmarried Child
Under 18, or 18 if in high school, or any age if disabled before age 22

When You Die Benefits May Be Paid To:

Your Spouse
Age 60 or over, or age 50-59 if disabled

Any age, if caring for your child who is under 16 or who is disabled before age 22

Your Unmarried Child
Under 18, or 18 if in high school, or any age if disabled before age 22

3 *What It Costs*

Who Pays

You and your employer each pay 6.2% in taxes for Social Security and 1.45% for Medicare Hospital Insurance. Your employer pays half the cost — you get all the benefits. Self-employed persons pay the combined employer-employee rate.

How Much

The taxes that you and your employer pay each year are based on:

- the tax rate (percent of pay) and
- the amount of your earnings taxed.

Current	Y-T-D	Deductions	Current	Y-T-D
$1,200.00	$27,600.00	FICA Tax Fed. Tax State Tax	$ 91.80 102.00 54.36	$2,111.40 2,346.00 1,250.28
$1,200.00	$27,600.00	Total Deductions	$248.16	$5,707.68

For Period Ending	NET PAY
11-12	$951.84

Two Taxes

Two separate payroll taxes are withheld from employees' wages:

- **Social Security:** This tax pays for monthly cash benefits to entitled beneficiaries.
- **Medicare (Hospital Insurance):** This tax pays for hospital insurance benefits for Medicare beneficiaries.

For most purposes, the two taxes are simply added together and treated as one amount — referred to as "payroll taxes" or **FICA** (Federal Insurance Contributions Act). Self-employed persons (who are responsible for both the employer and employee taxes) pay SECA (Self-Employment Contributions Act) taxes, which are reported on Schedule SE with their income tax returns.

You do not pay any Social Security tax on earnings over the **Maximum Taxable Amount** — $72,600 for 1999. There is no limit for Medicare.

Your Social Security tax equals the tax rate multiplied by your earnings (up to the Maximum Taxable Amount). Your employer pays the same amount on your behalf. **Tax Rates** are established by federal law.

The **Maximum Taxable Amount** for Social Security increases each year, based on increases in the average wages and salaries of all employees.

Examples — Payroll Taxes

Suppose you earn $30,000 in 1999. How much tax will be paid?

	Tax Rate		Earnings		Amount of Tax
You, Social Security	6.20%	×	$30,000	=	$1,860.00
You, Medicare	1.45%	×	30,000	=	435.00
			Your Total		$2,295.00
Employer, Social Security	6.20%	×	$30,000	=	$1,860.00
Employer, Medicare	1.45%	×	30,000	=	435.00
			Employer Total		$2,295.00
			Grand Total		$4,590.00

Suppose you earn $100,000 in 1999.

	Tax Rate		Taxable Amount		Amount of Tax
You, Social Security	6.20%	×	$ 72,600	=	$ 4,501.20
You, Medicare	1.45%	×	100,000	=	1,450.00
			Your Total		$ 5,951.20
Employer, Social Security	6.20%	×	$ 72,600	=	$ 4,501.20
Employer, Medicare	1.45%	×	100,000	=	1,450.00
			Employer Total		$ 5,951.20
			Grand Total		$11,902.40

Social Security and Medicare Taxes

Years	Employee and Employer Tax Rate	Self-Employed Tax Rate	Maximum Earnings Taxed Annually
1937-49	1.00%	Not Covered	$ 3,000
1950	1.50	Not Covered	3,000
1951-53	1.50	2.25%	3,600
1954	2.00	3.00	3,600
1955-56	2.00	3.00	4,200
1957-58	2.25	3.375	4,200
1959	2.50	3.75	4,800
1960-61	3.00	4.50	4,800
1962	3.125	4.70	4,800
1963-65	3.625	5.40	4,800
1966[a]	4.20	6.15	6,600
1967	4.40	6.40	6,600
1968	4.40	6.40	7,800
1969-70	4.80	6.90	7,800
1971	5.20	7.50	7,800
1972	5.20	7.50	9,000
1973	5.85	8.00	10,800
1974	5.85	7.90	13,200
1975	5.85	7.90	14,100
1976	5.85	7.90	15,300
1977	5.85	7.90	16,500
1978	6.05	8.10	17,700
1979	6.13	8.10	22,900
1980	6.13	8.10	25,900
1981	6.65	9.30	29,700
1982	6.70	9.35	32,400
1983	6.70	9.35	35,700
1984	6.70[b]	11.30	37,800
1985	7.05	11.80	39,600
1986	7.15	12.30	42,000
1987	7.15	12.30	43,800
1988	7.51	13.02	45,000
1989	7.51	13.02	48,000
1990	7.65	15.30[c]	51,300
1991	7.65	15.30[c]	53,400[d]
1992	7.65	15.30[c]	55,500[d]
1993	7.65	15.30[c]	57,600[d]
1994	7.65	15.30[c]	60,600[d]
1995	7.65	15.30[c]	61,200[d]
1996	7.65	15.30[c]	62,700[d]
1997	7.65	15.30[c]	65,400[d]
1998	7.65	15.30[c]	68,400[d]
1999	7.65	15.30[c]	72,600[d]

[a] Medicare started in 1966.   [b] Employers paid 7.00% in 1984.
[c] Half the tax is deductible as a business expense for federal income taxes.
[d] This is the maximum for Social Security. This figure will rise in the future as the national average wage rises. The maximum for Medicare was $125,000 in 1991, $130,200 in 1992, and $135,000 in 1993; no limit for subsequent years.

The following table shows the total Social Security taxes (but not Medicare taxes) paid by an employee who retires at the full retirement age of 65 at the beginning of various years. Earned income taxed for Social Security is assumed to have begun in the year that age 22 is reached. Three different earnings levels are shown.

	Total Social Security Taxes Paid by Employees[1] with Steady Work Records		
	If Your Earnings Were Equal To:		
Age 65 in Year	Maximum Taxable Amount or more	U.S. Average Earnings[2]	One-Half of U.S. Average Earnings
2000	$72,733	$32,608	$16,304
1999	68,242	30,823	15,412
1998	63,824	29,075	14,537
1997	59,656	27,382	13,691
1996	55,655	25,729	12,864
1995	51,821	24,167	12,083
1994	48,081	22,677	11,338
1993	44,369	21,242	10,621
1992	40,828	19,833	9,917
1991	37,417	18,435	9,217
1990	34,136	17,104	8,552
1989	30,985	15,819	7,910
1988	28,106	14,621	7,311
1987	25,409	13,468	6,734
1986	22,943	12,435	6,217
1985	20,579	11,462	5,731
1984	18,352	10,516	5,258
1983	16,340	9,657	4,828
1982	14,443	8,845	4,423
1981	12,723	8,071	4,036
1980	11,164	7,346	3,673
1979	9,848	6,710	3,355
1978	8,685	6,127	3,063
1977	7,791	5,594	2,797
1976	6,974	5,110	2,555
1975	6,217	4,653	2,326

[1] For 1990 and later, self-employed persons pay twice the amount that employees pay (but less than this before 1990).

[2] U.S. average earnings in 1998 is estimated to be $28,314; subsequent years are also estimates.

W-2 Form (Annual Earnings Report)

The W-2 form that you get from your employer shows the 6.2% Social Security tax separately from the 1.45% Medicare tax. This is because there is a maximum amount of earnings taxed for Social Security, but no maximum for Medicare (page 14).

a Control number 0001		Void ☐			
b Employer's identification number 13-2834414			**1** Wages, tips, other compensation 75,000.00		**2** Federal income tax withheld 9,175.00
c Employer's name, address, and ZIP code			**3** Social security wages 68,400.00		**4** Social security tax withheld 4,240.80
Grinstead Mfg. Co., Inc. 5701 Ringwood Drive Pittsburgh, Pennsylvania 15219			**5** Medicare wages and tips 75,000.00		**6** Medicare tax withheld 1,087.50
			7 Social security tips none		**8** Allocated tips none
d Employee's social security number 123-45-6789			**9** Advance EIC payment 0.00		**10** Dependent care benefits none
e Employee's name, address, and ZIP code			**11** Nonqualified plans none		**12** Benefits included in Box 1 430.20
John Q. Public 1907 Garden Court Pittsburgh, Pennsylvania 15270			**13**		**14** Other none
			15 Statutory employee ☐ Deceased ☐ Pension plan ☐ Legal rep ☐ 942 emp ☐ Subtotal ☐ Deferred compensation ☐		
16 State PA Employer's state I.D. No.	**17** State wages, tips, etc 75,000.00	**18** State income tax 2,840.00	**19** Locality name Pittsburgh	**20** Local wages, tips, etc 75,000.00	**21** Local income tax 1,132.00

Department of the Treasury—Internal Revenue Service

Form W-2 Wage and Tax Statement **1998**

Copy C For EMPLOYEE'S RECORDS (See Notice on back.)

Deductibility of Taxes
Social Security and Medicare taxes are not deductible for federal income taxes for employees, but half are for the self-employed.

What Is Taxed
All salaries, wages, bonuses, and commissions that you receive for working are taxed and credited to your earnings record. The Social Security tax is withheld until the Maximum Taxable Amount ($72,600 in 1999) for the year is reached. The Medicare tax is withheld from **every** paycheck.

In addition to cash payments, taxable amounts include the value of meals and lodging, except when they are provided for the convenience of your employer. The first six months of sick pay are taxed. The cost of employer-provided group term life insurance coverage exceeding $50,000 is also taxed. Employee contributions to "cash-or-deferred" plans under Section 401(k) of the Internal Revenue Code (IRC) are taxed, as are contributions to tax-deferred annuities under Section 403(b), even though federal income taxes on such amounts are deferred. This demonstrates that the rules for Social Security taxes and income taxes are not always the same.

If you have questions about what is taxable, call the IRS.

What Is Not Taxed

Payments from almost all employee benefit plans are excluded from payroll taxes, as are **employer** payments into such plans. Also, items of little value provided by your employer are generally not taxed. For example, you aren't taxed for using the company parking lot or medical clinic, or for discounts on company products. Contributions to a "flexible spending account" under IRC Section 125 are free of payroll and income taxes. Such plans permit an employee to authorize a salary reduction and use the money for such things as unreimbursed healthcare expenses and dependent care assistance.

Payroll Taxes on Non-Qualified Payments

Retired employees often receive a lump-sum payment, or a series of payments, outside of the qualified (IRS approved) retirement plan. These arrangements may be called deferred compensation plans, supplemental executive retirement programs (SERPs), severance payments, or some other name. The Social Security and Medicare tax rules for such payments are complicated, but here are some fundamentals. If the agreement includes a "substantial risk of forfeiture," such as a provision prohibiting competition, then the taxes apply as the payments are made.

Where no "substantial risk of forfeiture" exists, then the tax is payable in the year that the right to the money becomes fixed or vested. This means that the present value of the future payments must be determined. The IRS has not issued final regulations on this, but it has been accepting employer determinations that are reasonable.

If the retiree has already paid the maximum tax for the year that the non-qualified benefit became vested, there is no need to make the calculation. But the problem has been complicated by the removal of the ceiling on the taxable wage base for the Medicare portion of the tax for years beginning with 1994. While many recipients of non-qualified payments will have had regular salary payments which exceeded the taxable wage base for Social Security ($72,600 in 1999) — they will still have to pay the 1.45% Medicare tax on the value of the non-qualified payment if the benefit became vested after 1993.

Director Fees

Special Social Security and Medicare tax rules apply to fees paid to members of corporate boards of directors. Such fees are classified as self-employment income.

Ordinarily, self-employment income is taxable for Social Security and Medicare and counts against the earnings limitation when you receive it. However, for corporate directors the law is slightly different. Director fees count against the earnings limitation when they are earned, even if the director chooses to defer payment until later. This means a director cannot collect Social Security benefits while **earning** substantial fees. In 1988-90, Social Security and Medicare taxes were also paid on deferred director fees when earned, but starting in 1991 taxes have been payable on director fees **when received.**

Domestic Service

In 1999, wages of $1,100 or more per year paid to workers age 18 and over to work at an employer's home are subject to Social Security and Medicare payroll taxes. Only payments in money are subject to these taxes for this type of work — not material things such as meals. The law exempts household workers under 18 who are students, or who have another occupation which is their principal one.

Agricultural Labor

If you are paid $150 or more in a calendar year from one employer for farm work or if that employer pays at least $2,500 to all employees for labor during the year, you are generally subject to payroll taxes, and your earnings will count in figuring your benefits.

Tips

If you receive tips of $20 or more in a month, all of your cash tips are treated as regular wages.

Two or More Employers

If you work for more than one employer in a year, **each one** must withhold Medicare taxes on all of your earnings, and up to the Maximum Taxable Amount for Social Security. If your **total earnings** from all employers are more than the maximum, then you will have paid too much Social Security tax.

What happens when you overpay? You can credit the overpayment against the federal income taxes that you owe for that year when you file your return, or you can claim a refund (page 177). Your employers do not get a credit or refund for their payments.

Family Employment

If you are self-employed and hire your spouse, parent, or child age 18 or older **in the course of your business,** this is covered employment. If the employment is not in the course of your business, this is **not** covered.

Self-Employed

If you are self-employed, you are covered by Social Security and Medicare, except for ministers who, at ordination, can opt out on grounds of conscience or religious principles.

As a self-employed person, you are entitled to a deduction in computing net earnings to reflect the fact that employees do not pay FICA taxes on the value of the **employer's** matching tax. Accordingly, you deduct from net earnings from self-employment, an amount equal to one-half of the self-employment tax on such earnings, at a rate of 15.3%. This means that you pay the tax on 92.35% of your net annual income from self-employment (if the result is at least $400). This amount is considered your self-employment income for benefit purposes.

In general, net income is figured under the same rules as for income tax purposes. You determine your payroll taxes on self-employment income using tax form (Schedule SE). Also, you deduct half of your Social Security and Medicare self-employment tax as a business expense on your income tax return.

If you are in more than one type of self-employment, the profits and losses of all businesses are added together to figure your net income.

If you are both self-employed and an employee, you pay taxes on your employee earnings at the employee tax rate. The following rules apply:

- If you **earn the Maximum Taxable Amount (or more)** for Social Security as an employee, you do not pay any Social Security self-employment tax.

- If you earn **less than the Maximum Taxable Amount** as an employee, you must pay the Social Security self-employment tax on the amount of your self-employment earnings (after adjustment by the 92.35% factor — page 22) that brings you up to the maximum, when added to your wages as an employee. You do not pay self-employment taxes on any amount above the maximum.

- You pay **Medicare tax,** on *all* of your earnings as an employee, and from self-employment (after the 92.35% adjustment).

You must pay the Social Security tax even if you don't have to pay any federal income tax. If a husband and wife file a joint income tax return, each one who has self-employment income must file his or her own Schedule SE.

The Tax Rates and Maximum Taxable Amounts for the self-employed are shown on page 16.

Benefits for the Self Employed

Benefits for the self employed are the same as for employees.

Taxes after Benefits Begin

If you work while receiving benefits, you still pay Social Security and Medicare taxes on your earnings.

Some or all Social Security benefits in a year may be suspended if earned income exceeds the earnings limitation (see pages 54-58).

Although Social Security benefits are tax-free for most people, those with high total incomes must include up to 85% of their benefits as income for federal income tax purposes. Special step-rate "thresholds" determine the amount on which you may be taxed:

- Single persons: $25,000 and $34,000.
- Married couples filing a joint return: $32,000 and $44,000.
- Married couples filing separate returns and living together at any time during the year have zero thresholds (if not living together, they are considered as single persons).

The Preliminary Adjusted Gross Income (earnings, pensions, dividends and taxable interest from investments, and other sources), *plus* interest on tax-exempt bonds, *plus* 50% of Social Security benefits is compared with these thresholds. Fifty percent of any excess over the first threshold, plus 35% of any excess over the second threshold is included in Adjusted Gross Income. This amount cannot exceed the smaller of (a) 85% of the benefits or (b) 50% of the benefits, plus 85% of any excess over the second threshold.

For Social Security beneficiaries who are subject to federal income taxes, part or all of such taxes can voluntarily be withheld from the monthly benefit. Decide what percentage (7, 15, 28 or 31) you want withheld. Complete IRS form W-4V, and submit it to you local Social Security office.

Examples of Federal Income Taxes on Social Security Benefits

Single Person with $10,000/Year in Benefits

Preliminary Adjusted Gross Income (PAGI)	$31,000
Tax-free bond interest	2,000
50% of $10,000 in Social Security benefit	5,000
Modified Adjusted Gross Income (MAGI)	$38,000
Excess of MAGI over first threshold ($25,000)	$13,000
Excess of MAGI over second threshold ($34,000)	$ 4,000

(1) 50% of MAGI over 1st threshold, plus 35% of
     MAGI over 2nd threshold
     (.50 × $13,000 + .35 × $4,000) . . . . **$ 7,900**
(2) 85% of benefits (.85 × $10,000) . . . . $ 8,500
(3) 50% of benefits, plus 85% of MAGI over 2nd
     threshold (.50 × $10,000 + .85 × $4,000) . . . . $ 8,400

The smallest of these three figures, $7,900, is added to the PAGI of $31,000, making the Adjusted Gross Income $38,900.

Married Couple with $20,000/Year in Benefits

Preliminary Adjusted Gross Income (PAGI)	$50,000
Tax-free bond interest	2,000
50% of $20,000 in Social Security benefits	10,000
Modified Adjusted Gross Income (MAGI)	$62,000
Excess of MAGI over first threshold ($32,000)	$30,000
Excess of MAGI over second threshold ($44,000)	$18,000

(1) 50% of MAGI over 1st threshold, plus 35% of
     MAGI over 2nd threshold
     (.50 × $30,000 + .35 × $18,000) $21,300
(2) 85% of benefits (.85 × $20,000) **$17,000**
(3) 50% of benefits, plus 85% of MAGI over 2nd
     threshold (.50 × $20,000 + .85 × $18,000) $25,300

The smallest of these three figures, $17,000, is added to the PAGI of $50,000, making the Adjusted Gross Income $67,000.

Most states do not tax Social Security benefits, but you should consult your tax advisor.

4 *Retirement Benefits*

All monthly benefits are based on your **Primary Insurance Amount** (PIA) which is the amount you would receive if you retired at your **Full Retirement Age** (FRA), currently age 65. (For persons born after 1937, the FRA will gradually increase, see page 44.) The PIA calculation is described on pages 31-42, 151.

Easy-Reference Table

The following table shows approximate monthly benefits at age 65 for you and your spouse. It is assumed that you have worked steadily and received pay raises at a rate equal to the U.S. average throughout your working career. It is also assumed that your earnings and the general level of wages and salaries in the country will stay the same until you retire. This way, **the table shows the value of your benefits in today's dollars.**

Your spouse may, instead, qualify for a higher retirement benefit based on her or his own work record.

Monthly Benefits at Age 65

Your Age in 1999	Who Receives Benefits	Your Present Annual Earnings				
		$20,000	$30,000	$45,000	$60,000	$72,600 and Up
65	You	$736	$969	$1,216	$1,316	$1,373
	Spouse	368	484	608	658	686
64	You	744	980	1,233	1,338	1,400
	Spouse	372	490	616	669	700
63	You	763	1,006	1,268	1,381	1,448
	Spouse	381	503	634	690	724
62	You	795	1,047	1,326	1,448	1,521
	Spouse	397	523	663	724	760
61*	You	788	1,037	1,315	1,441	1,518
	Spouse	392	517	655	718	756
55*	You	749	986	1,257	1,406	1,504
	Spouse	367	484	617	690	739
50*	You	753	993	1,262	1,430	1,549
	Spouse	370	487	620	702	761
45*	You	758	1,000	1,267	1,437	1,572
	Spouse	372	491	622	706	772
40*	You	717	947	1,196	1,358	1,491
	Spouse	346	457	577	655	719
35*	You	712	941	1,185	1,346	1,482
	Spouse	342	452	569	647	712
30*	You	715	947	1,189	1,352	1,488
	Spouse	344	455	571	650	715

*These amounts have been reduced for retirement at age 65 because the FRA is higher for these persons (see pages 46-47 and 153).

Starting with the year you turn 62, your benefits are increased to reflect changes in the cost of living, whether or not you are retired. These increases are effective every December and are normally payable to beneficiaries in January. They are included in the table for persons who became age 62 before 1999. No cost-of-living increases are included for December 1999 or later.

A **Maximum Family Benefit** applies if more than two persons receive payments on the same Social Security record (page 66).

The table on page 27 shows only **approximate** retirement benefits. For a more accurate figure, follow the steps on pages 31-42. For an exact figure, you need your entire earnings history, which you can obtain by completing and mailing Form SSA-7004 in the back of this book.

Benefits as a Percentage of Pay

The table on page 27 gives you a close estimate of your age-65 benefit in today's dollars. Inflation would cause the actual dollars to be much higher, however. The graph on page 29 illustrates the benefit at FRA as a percentage of pay **subject to the Social Security tax** in the year before you retire. It applies to anyone who has had **steady** earnings.

Find your annual pay on the graph. For example, if you earn $35,000, find it on the bottom (horizontal) line of the chart. Reading up to the graph line and over to the vertical line on the left side reveals that you could expect a benefit of 39% of your final level of pay. If no future inflation occurs, your annual benefit would be about $13,600 per year (39% × $35,000).

If your earnings are equal to the U.S. average (about $30,000 now), you can expect to receive a benefit of about 41% of pay. If you always had maximum taxable earnings, you can expect to receive about 25% of that **portion** of your pay subject to the Social Security tax (gradually increasing to 28% after 2010). The **replacement ratio** refers to the percentage of your pay that is replaced by your Social Security retirement benefit.

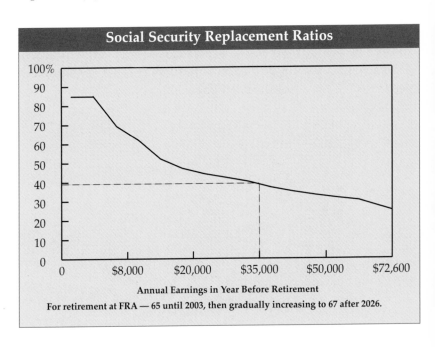

Social Security Replacement Ratios

Annual Earnings in Year Before Retirement

For retirement at FRA — 65 until 2003, then gradually increasing to 67 after 2026.

Qualifications for Retirement Benefits

To qualify for retirement benefits, you must be **fully insured;** that is, you must have the required number of **credits** under Social Security. Most workers need 40 credits to qualify for retirement benefits — or about 10 years of work. For each birth year before 1929, one less credit is required (but no fewer than six).

Through 1977, you earned one credit for any calendar quarter in which you had wages or salary of at least $50 in covered employment. Four credits are earned for any calendar year in which covered self-employment earnings were at least $400 (but at most four credits for any one year). Since 1978, you earn credits on the basis of your annual earnings, up to four credits in any year. In **1999,** one credit is recorded for every **$740** you earn during the year, with four credits if you earn $2,960 or more. The amount increases each year based on wage inflation. (The amounts required to earn a credit in 1978-99 are shown in column G of the worksheet on page 34.)

How To Figure Your Retirement Benefit Amount

Your retirement benefit is based on your **Primary Insurance Amount (PIA).** To figure your PIA, you need to know your **Average Indexed Monthly Earnings (AIME),** which is based on your lifetime earnings history. If you were born in 1937 or later, you can figure your own AIME by following the steps on the next page and using the worksheet on page 34. If you were born before 1937, use the appropriate worksheet that follows (see pages 39-46). (If you were born on January 1, refer to the year prior to the year of your birth.) This will enable you to make a good estimate of your PIA. Of course, to get a completely accurate PIA, you need your entire earnings history right up to the time of your retirement.

The PIA is the amount payable to you at your Full Retirement Age, which is 65 for persons born before 1938. If you retire earlier, your benefit will be less than the PIA (pages 48-55). If you retire later, it will be more than the PIA (pages 55-56).

How To Figure Your AIME and PIA:

(1) In column C of the worksheet for your year of birth, enter your earnings for each year after 1950. **You can get this information from the Earnings and Benefit Estimate Statement** that you can request from the Social Security Administration (page 176). If your earnings for any year were more than the Maximum Taxable Amount, use the maximum.

(2) On the last two lines of column C, enter your expected earnings for 1999 and for all **future** years that you plan to work after 1999. Assume future earnings to be the same as 1999, so that your benefit will be more closely related to the value of today's dollar. Remember that higher earnings resulting from the increase in the cost of living will be balanced by higher costs generally. If you are 62 in 1999 or earlier, do not consider earnings after 1998 when figuring the benefit payable in 1999.

(3) Multiply the earnings for all years by the Index Factors in column D. The index factors make past earnings comparable to the level of earnings today. Enter the results of your multiplication in column E, Indexed Earnings.

(4) If you were born after January 1, 1929, use the 35 best years of earnings (after indexing) to figure your AIME. If you have fewer than 35 years of earnings, use zero for each of the remaining years.

Note: For Social Security (and Medicare) purposes, you "reach an age" on the day before your birthday. Thus, if you were born on January 1, you are in essence considered to have been born in the previous year.

(5) On the worksheet, put check marks in column F by the years of your highest indexed earnings shown in column E. Continue until you have checked 35 years. For the "2000+" box, write the number of years that it represents, if this is a high year.

(6) Add up all the indexed earnings in column E for the years you have checked in column F. (If the "2000+" line is to be used, multiply the number in column F by the earnings in column E and use the result in the addition.)
. . . . $ _____

(7) Multiply the number of years in step 4 by 12 to get months.
. . . .   _____

(8) Divide the total earnings shown in step 6 by the months shown in step 7 to get your AIME (drop cents).
. . . . $ _____

Now, to figure your PIA:
(9) If you were born in 1937 or later, look at the table on pages 84-85. Find the number in the first column that is closest to your AIME. The numbers on this line are your approximate PIA and the other benefits based on it.

For a more precise benefit determination, apply the 1999 benefit formula shown on page 151. The benefit amount is increased by the cost-of-living percentage effective for December of the year in which you reach age 62 and for all subsequent years, whether or not you have actually retired.

If you were born in 1929-1936, use the benefit formula for your age shown on page 151.

Worksheet for Figuring Indexed Earnings *only* if Born in 1937 or later

A Calendar Year	B Maximum Taxable Amount	C Enter Your Taxable Earnings ×	D Index Factor =	E Indexed Earnings	F High Years	G Earnings Required for a Credit
1951	$3,600		9.79794			$50
1952	3,600		9.22403			50
1953	3,600		8.73595			50
1954	3,600		8.69111			50
1955	4,200		8.30728			50
1956	4,200		7.76421			50
1957	4,200		7.53106			50
1958	4,200		7.46529			50
1959	4,800		7.11292			50
1960	4,800		6.84432			50
1961	4,800		6.71094			50
1962	4,800		6.39092			50
1963	4,800		6.23795			50
1964	4,800		5.99302			50
1965	4,800		5.88702			50
1966	6,600		5.55367			50
1967	6,600		5.26063			50
1968	7,800		4.92232			50
1969	7,800		4.65340			50
1970	7,800		4.43339			50
1971	7,800		4.22128			50
1972	9,000		3.84451			50
1973	10,800		3.61813			50
1974	13,200		3.41512			50
1975	14,100		3.17765			50
1976	15,300		2.97253			50
1977	16,500		2.80446			50
1978	17,700		2.59814			250
1979	22,900		2.38914			260
1980	25,900		2.19172			290
1981	29,700		1.99127			310
1982	32,400		1.88737			340
1983	35,700		1.79970			370
1984	37,800		1.69978			390
1985	39,600		1.63032			410
1986	42,000		1.58332			440
1987	43,800		1.48840			460
1988	45,000		1.41853			470
1989	48,000		1.36451			500
1990	51,300		1.30426			520
1991	53,400		1.25740			540
1992	55,500		1.19579			570
1993	57,600		1.18560			590
1994	60,600		1.15461			620
1995	61,200		1.11011			630
1996	62,700		1.05835			640
1997	65,400		1.00000			670
1998	68,400		1.00000			700
1999	72,600		1.00000			740
2000+	*		1.00000			*

*To be determined (see page 14 as to column B and page 30 as to column G).
Note: Index factors change each year based on U.S. average wage.

Worksheet for Figuring Your Indexed Earnings *only* if Born in 1936

A Calendar Year	B Maximum Taxable Amount	C Enter Your Taxable Earnings	×	D Index Factor	=	E Indexed Earnings	F High Years
1951	$ 3,600			9.25774			
1952	3,600			8.71548			
1953	3,600			8.25431			
1954	3,600			8.21193			
1955	4,200			7.84927			
1956	4,200			7.33614			
1957	4,200			7.11584			
1958	4,200			7.05370			
1959	4,800			6.72076			
1960	4,800			6.46696			
1961	4,800			6.34094			
1962	4,800			6.03857			
1963	4,800			5.89402			
1964	4,800			5.66261			
1965	4,800			5.56245			
1966	6,600			5.24747			
1967	6,600			4.97060			
1968	7,800			4.65094			
1969	7,800			4.39684			
1970	7,800			4.18896			
1971	7,800			3.98855			
1972	9,000			3.63255			
1973	10,800			3.41865			
1974	13,200			3.22683			
1975	14,100			3.00245			
1976	15,300			2.80864			
1977	16,500			2.64983			
1978	17,700			2.45489			
1979	22,900			2.25741			
1980	25,900			2.07088			
1981	29,700			1.88149			
1982	32,400			1.78331			
1983	35,700			1.70047			
1984	37,800			1.60606			
1985	39,600			1.54043			
1986	42,000			1.49603			
1987	43,800			1.40634			
1988	45,000			1.34033			
1989	48,000			1.28928			
1990	51,300			1.23235			
1991	53,400			1.18808			
1992	55,500			1.12986			
1993	57,600			1.12023			
1994	60,600			1.09095			
1995	61,200			1.04891			
1996	62,700			1.00000			
1997	65,400			1.00000			
1998	68,400			1.00000			
1999	72,600			1.00000			
2000+	*			1.00000			

*To be determined.

Worksheet for Figuring Your Indexed Earnings *only* if Born in 1935

A Calendar Year	B Maximum Taxable Amount	C Enter Your Taxable Earnings	×	D Index Factor	=	E Indexed Earnings	F High Years
1951	$ 3,600			8.82610			
1952	3,600			8.30912			
1953	3,600			7.86945			
1954	3,600			7.82905			
1955	4,200			7.48330			
1956	4,200			6.99409			
1957	4,200			6.78406			
1958	4,200			6.72482			
1959	4,800			6.40740			
1960	4,800			6.16544			
1961	4,800			6.04529			
1962	4,800			5.75702			
1963	4,800			5.61921			
1964	4,800			5.39859			
1965	4,800			5.30310			
1966	6,600			5.00281			
1967	6,600			4.73884			
1968	7,800			4.43409			
1969	7,800			4.19183			
1970	7,800			3.99365			
1971	7,800			3.80258			
1972	9,000			3.46318			
1973	10,800			3.25925			
1974	13,200			3.07638			
1975	14,100			2.86246			
1976	15,300			2.67769			
1977	16,500			2.52629			
1978	17,700			2.34043			
1979	22,900			2.15216			
1980	25,900			1.97433			
1981	29,700			1.79376			
1982	32,400			1.70016			
1983	35,700			1.62119			
1984	37,800			1.53118			
1985	39,600			1.46861			
1986	42,000			1.42627			
1987	43,800			1.34077			
1988	45,000			1.27783			
1989	48,000			1.22916			
1990	51,300			1.17489			
1991	53,400			1.13268			
1992	55,500			1.07718			
1993	57,600			1.06800			
1994	60,600			1.04008			
1995	61,200			1.00000			
1996	62,700			1.00000			
1997	65,400			1.00000			
1998	68,400			1.00000			
1999	72,600			1.00000			
2000+	*			1.00000			

*To be determined.

Worksheet for Figuring Your Indexed Earnings *only* if Born in 1934

A Calendar Year	B Maximum Taxable Amount	C Enter Your Taxable Earnings	×	D Index Factor	=	E Indexed Earnings	F High Years
1951	$3,600			8.48595			
1952	3,600			7.98889			
1953	3,600			7.56617			
1954	3,600			7.52733			
1955	4,200			7.19490			
1956	4,200			6.72455			
1957	4,200			6.52261			
1958	4,200			6.46566			
1959	4,800			6.16047			
1960	4,800			5.92783			
1961	4,800			5.81231			
1962	4,800			5.53515			
1963	4,800			5.40266			
1964	4,800			5.19053			
1965	4,800			5.09872			
1966	6,600			4.81000			
1967	6,600			4.55621			
1968	7,800			4.26320			
1969	7,800			4.03028			
1970	7,800			3.83974			
1971	7,800			3.65603			
1972	9,000			3.32972			
1973	10,800			3.13364			
1974	13,200			2.95782			
1975	14,100			2.75214			
1976	15,300			2.57450			
1977	16,500			2.42893			
1978	17,700			2.25023			
1979	22,900			2.06922			
1980	25,900			1.89824			
1981	29,700			1.72463			
1982	32,400			1.63464			
1983	35,700			1.55871			
1984	37,800			1.47217			
1985	39,600			1.41201			
1986	42,000			1.37131			
1987	43,800			1.28910			
1988	45,000			1.22859			
1989	48,000			1.18179			
1990	51,300			1.12962			
1991	53,400			1.08903			
1992	55,500			1.03567			
1993	57,600			1.02684			
1994	60,600			1.00000			
1995	61,200			1.00000			
1996	62,700			1.00000			
1997	65,400			1.00000			
1998	68,400			1.00000			
1999	72,600			1.00000			
2000+	*			1.00000			

*To be determined.

Worksheet for Figuring Your Indexed Earnings *only* if Born in 1933

A	B	C		D		E	F
Calendar Year	Maximum Taxable Amount	Enter Your Taxable Earnings	×	Index Factor	=	Indexed Earnings	High Years
1951	$ 3,600			8.26415			
1952	3,600			7.78008			
1953	3,600			7.36841			
1954	3,600			7.33058			
1955	4,200			7.00684			
1956	4,200			6.54879			
1957	4,200			6.35213			
1958	4,200			6.29666			
1959	4,800			5.99945			
1960	4,800			5.77289			
1961	4,800			5.66039			
1962	4,800			5.39047			
1963	4,800			5.26144			
1964	4,800			5.05486			
1965	4,800			4.96546			
1966	6,600			4.68428			
1967	6,600			4.43712			
1968	7,800			4.15177			
1969	7,800			3.92494			
1970	7,800			3.73937			
1971	7,800			3.56047			
1972	9,000			3.24269			
1973	10,800			3.05174			
1974	13,200			2.88051			
1975	14,100			2.68021			
1976	15,300			2.50720			
1977	16,500			2.36544			
1978	17,700			2.19142			
1979	22,900			2.01514			
1980	25,900			1.84862			
1981	29,700			1.67955			
1982	32,400			1.59192			
1983	35,700			1.51797			
1984	37,800			1.43369			
1985	39,600			1.37510			
1986	42,000			1.33546			
1987	43,800			1.25540			
1988	45,000			1.19647			
1989	48,000			1.15090			
1990	51,300			1.10009			
1991	53,400			1.06057			
1992	55,500			1.00860			
1993	57,600			1.00000			
1994	60,600			1.00000			
1995	61,200			1.00000			
1996	62,700			1.00000			
1997	65,400			1.00000			
1998	68,400			1.00000			
1999	72,600			1.00000			
2000+	*			1.00000			

*To be determined.

Worksheet for Figuring Your Indexed Earnings *only* if Born in 1932

A Calendar Year	B Maximum Taxable Amount	C Enter Your Taxable Earnings	×	D Index Factor	=	E Indexed Earnings	F High Years
1951	$ 3,600			8.19368			
1952	3,600			7.71374			
1953	3,600			7.30558			
1954	3,600			7.26807			
1955	4,200			6.94710			
1956	4,200			6.49295			
1957	4,200			6.29796			
1958	4,200			6.24297			
1959	4,800			5.94829			
1960	4,800			5.72367			
1961	4,800			5.61213			
1962	4,800			5.34451			
1963	4,800			5.21658			
1964	4,800			5.01176			
1965	4,800			4.92312			
1966	6,600			4.64434			
1967	6,600			4.39929			
1968	7,800			4.11637			
1969	7,800			3.89148			
1970	7,800			3.70749			
1971	7,800			3.53011			
1972	9,000			3.21504			
1973	10,800			3.02572			
1974	13,200			2.85595			
1975	14,100			2.65736			
1976	15,300			2.48583			
1977	16,500			2.34527			
1978	17,700			2.17273			
1979	22,900			1.99795			
1980	25,900			1.83286			
1981	29,700			1.66523			
1982	32,400			1.57834			
1983	35,700			1.50502			
1984	37,800			1.42146			
1985	39,600			1.36338			
1986	42,000			1.32408			
1987	43,800			1.24470			
1988	45,000			1.18627			
1989	48,000			1.14109			
1990	51,300			1.09071			
1991	53,400			1.05152			
1992	55,500			1.00000			
1993	57,600			1.00000			
1994	60,600			1.00000			
1995	61,200			1.00000			
1996	62,700			1.00000			
1997	65,400			1.00000			
1998	68,400			1.00000			
1999	72,600			1.00000			
2000+	*			1.00000			

*To be determined.

Worksheet for Figuring Your Indexed Earnings *only* if Born in 1931

A Calendar Year	B Maximum Taxable Amount	C Enter Your Taxable Earnings	×	D Index Factor	=	E Indexed Earnings	F High Years
1951	$ 3,600			7.79219			
1952	3,600			7.33577			
1953	3,600			6.94761			
1954	3,600			6.91194			
1955	4,200			6.60669			
1956	4,200			6.17480			
1957	4,200			5.98937			
1958	4,200			5.93707			
1959	4,800			5.65683			
1960	4,800			5.44321			
1961	4,800			5.33714			
1962	4,800			5.08263			
1963	4,800			4.96097			
1964	4,800			4.76619			
1965	4,800			4.68189			
1966	6,600			4.41677			
1967	6,600			4.18373			
1968	7,800			3.91467			
1969	7,800			3.70080			
1970	7,800			3.52583			
1971	7,800			3.35714			
1972	9,000			3.05750			
1973	10,800			2.87746			
1974	13,200			2.71601			
1975	14,100			2.52715			
1976	15,300			2.36402			
1977	16,500			2.23035			
1978	17,700			2.06627			
1979	22,900			1.90005			
1980	25,900			1.74305			
1981	29,700			1.58364			
1982	32,400			1.50100			
1983	35,700			1.43128			
1984	37,800			1.35181			
1985	39,600			1.29657			
1986	42,000			1.25920			
1987	43,800			1.18371			
1988	45,000			1.12814			
1989	48,000			1.08518			
1990	51,300			1.03727			
1991	53,400			1.00000			
1992	55,500			1.00000			
1993	57,600			1.00000			
1994	60,600			1.00000			
1995	61,200			1.00000			
1996	62,700			1.00000			
1997	65,400			1.00000			
1998	68,400			1.00000			
1999	72,600			1.00000			
2000+	*			1.00000			

*To be determined.

Worksheet for Figuring Your Indexed Earnings *only* if Born in 1930

A Calendar Year	B Maximum Taxable Amount	C Enter Your Taxable Earnings	×	D Index Factor	=	E Indexed Earnings	F High Years
1951	$ 3,600			7.51225			
1952	3,600			7.07222			
1953	3,600			6.69800			
1954	3,600			6.66362			
1955	4,200			6.36934			
1956	4,200			5.95295			
1957	4,200			5.77419			
1958	4,200			5.72377			
1959	4,800			5.45360			
1960	4,800			5.24765			
1961	4,800			5.14539			
1962	4,800			4.90003			
1963	4,800			4.78274			
1964	4,800			4.59495			
1965	4,800			4.51368			
1966	6,600			4.25809			
1967	6,600			4.03342			
1968	7,800			3.77403			
1969	7,800			3.56784			
1970	7,800			3.39915			
1971	7,800			3.23653			
1972	9,000			2.94765			
1973	10,800			2.77408			
1974	13,200			2.61843			
1975	14,100			2.43635			
1976	15,300			2.27909			
1977	16,500			2.15022			
1978	17,700			1.99203			
1979	22,900			1.83179			
1980	25,900			1.68043			
1981	29,700			1.52674			
1982	32,400			1.44708			
1983	35,700			1.37986			
1984	37,800			1.30325			
1985	39,600			1.24999			
1986	42,000			1.21396			
1987	43,800			1.14118			
1988	45,000			1.08761			
1989	48,000			1.04619			
1990	51,300			1.00000			
1991	53,400			1.00000			
1992	55,500			1.00000			
1993	57,600			1.00000			
1994	60,600			1.00000			
1995	61,200			1.00000			
1996	62,700			1.00000			
1997	65,400			1.00000			
1998	68,400			1.00000			
1999	72,600			1.00000			
2000+	*			1.00000			

*To be determined.

Worksheet for Figuring Your Indexed Earnings *only* if Born in 1929

A Calendar Year	B Maximum Taxable Amount	C Enter Your Taxable Earnings	×	D Index Factor	=	E Indexed Earnings	F High Years
1951	$ 3,600			7.18056			
1952	3,600			6.75997			
1953	3,600			6.40227			
1954	3,600			6.36941			
1955	4,200			6.08812			
1956	4,200			5.69012			
1957	4,200			5.51925			
1958	4,200			5.47105			
1959	4,800			5.21281			
1960	4,800			5.01596			
1961	4,800			4.91821			
1962	4,800			4.68368			
1963	4,800			4.57157			
1964	4,800			4.39208			
1965	4,800			4.31439			
1966	6,600			4.07009			
1967	6,600			3.85533			
1968	7,800			3.60740			
1969	7,800			3.41031			
1970	7,800			3.24907			
1971	7,800			3.09363			
1972	9,000			2.81751			
1973	10,800			2.65160			
1974	13,200			2.50282			
1975	14,100			2.32878			
1976	15,300			2.17846			
1977	16,500			2.05529			
1978	17,700			1.90408			
1979	22,900			1.75091			
1980	25,900			1.60623			
1981	29,700			1.45933			
1982	32,400			1.38319			
1983	35,700			1.31893			
1984	37,800			1.24571			
1985	39,600			1.19480			
1986	42,000			1.16036			
1987	43,800			1.09080			
1988	45,000			1.03959			
1989	48,000			1.00000			
1990	51,300			1.00000			
1991	53,400			1.00000			
1992	55,500			1.00000			
1993	57,600			1.00000			
1994	60,600			1.00000			
1995	61,200			1.00000			
1996	62,700			1.00000			
1997	65,400			1.00000			
1998	68,400			1.00000			
1999	72,600			1.00000			
2000+	*			1.00000			

*To be determined.

Minimum Retirement Benefits

Special-Minimum Benefit (Long Service at Low Earnings)

Workers who have many years of work under Social Security, but at low earnings, may qualify for a **special-minimum benefit.** The amount of the PIA for this benefit depends on the number of years of "significant" Social Security coverage. Here's how that PIA is figured:

For 1937-50, divide your total earnings by $900 to obtain your years of coverage (maximum 14). For 1951-78, you were credited for each year that you earned at least 25% of the Maximum Taxable Earnings. For 1979-90, you are credited for each year that you earned about 19% of the Maximum Taxable Earnings. After 1990, you are credited with a year of coverage if you earned about 11% of the maximum. For 1999, you will be credited with a year of coverage if you earn at least $8,055.

For December 1998 through November 1999, the special-minimum benefit is *approximately* $28.30 per month for each year of coverage **over 10 years — up to 30 years.** Thus, for 11 years of coverage, the special-minimum PIA is $27.90, while for 30 or more years of coverage, it is $567.00.

For those retiring before the Full Retirement Age, the benefit is reduced by applying reduction factors to the PIA (see pages 45-48). However, for those delaying retirement after such age, no Delayed Retirement Credits are given when computing the special-minimum benefit (see page 49).

The special-minimum benefit is paid only if it is higher than the benefit calculated under the regular rules, described previously, and this is seldom the case. The Social Security Administration automatically calculates your benefit, using both methods, and pays whichever is higher.

Full Retirement Age

Beginning with persons born in 1938, the Full Retirement Age will gradually increase from age 65, eventually reaching age 67 for persons born after 1959. The benefit at the Full Retirement Age is the Primary Insurance Amount (page 26).

The following table illustrates this important provision:

Full Retirement Age for Retired Worker and Spouses' Benefits	Year of Birth	Full Retirement Age for Surviving Spouses' Benefits
65	Before 1938	65
65 and 2 months	1938	65
65 and 4 months	1939	65
65 and 6 months	1940	65 and 2 months
65 and 8 months	1941	65 and 4 months
65 and 10 months	1942	65 and 6 months
66	1943	65 and 8 months
66	1944	65 and 10 months
66	1945-54	66
66 and 2 months	1955	66
66 and 4 months	1956	66
66 and 6 months	1957	66 and 2 months
66 and 8 months	1958	66 and 4 months
66 and 10 months	1959	66 and 6 months
67	1960	66 and 8 months
67	1961	66 and 10 months
67	1962 and after	67

Note: If you were born on January 1, refer to the year prior to the year of your birth.

Early Retirement

You can claim retirement benefits as early as the first **full** month that you are age 62 if you are fully insured (page 30). You will have a smaller monthly benefit though for the rest of your life, than if you wait until the Full Retirement Age (FRA).

It will be smaller for two reasons. First, you will probably have lower average earnings because you won't have the earnings of later years. Second, you will receive more monthly benefit payments because they will begin sooner. Accordingly, the benefit is permanently reduced. This way, the total benefits you receive will have about the same value assuming that you live to an average age.

How much your benefit will be reduced for early retirement depends on your age when the benefits begin. On the following page are reduced benefits for certain ages and PIAs for persons **born before 1938.** The reductions are somewhat larger for persons born after 1937, as discussed later. For example, for persons born in 1943-54, the FRA is 66 and the reduced benefit at 62 is 75% of the PIA. For persons born after 1959, the FRA is 67 and the reduced benefit at 62 is 70% of the PIA.

Examples of Your Reduced Benefits at Early Retirement for Persons Born Before 1938

If You Retire at Age	You Will Receive This Percent of Your PIA	You Will Receive This Benefit if Your PIA Is:		
		$600	$900	$1,300
65	100	$600	$900	$1,300
64½	96⅔	580	870	1,256
64	93⅓	560	840	1,213
63½	90	540	810	1,170
63	86⅔	520	780	1,126
62½	83⅓	500	750	1,083
62	80	480	720	1,040

You may retire at ages between the ones shown. The reduction factor applied to the PIA is $\frac{5}{9}$ of 1% for each of the first 36 months that commencement is prior to the FRA, plus $\frac{5}{12}$ of 1% for each such month in excess of 36. These reduction factors are for workers only.

For **spouse's benefits,** start with an amount equal to 50% of the worker's PIA. Then apply a reduction factor of $\frac{25}{36}$ of 1% for each of the first 36 months that commencement is prior to the spouse's Full Retirement Age, plus $\frac{5}{12}$ of 1% for each such month in excess of 36 (see tables on page 48). A spouse's reduction is slightly larger than that of the worker because of a contingent benefit for which there is a cost — that is, on the death of the worker, the reduction no longer applies. Then, the spouse will be paid a much larger benefit — generally, an amount equal to the worker's benefit (pages 90-92).

Age Benefits Begin	Percentage of Worker's PIA Received	You Will Receive This Benefit if Worker's PIA Is:		
		$600	$900	$1,300
65	50	$300	$450	$650
64½	47.92	288	431	623
64	45.83	275	412	596
63½	43.75	263	394	569
63	41.67	250	375	542
62½	39.59	238	356	515
62	37.50	225	338	488

Example of Spouse's Reduced Benefits at Early Retirement for Persons Born Before 1938

Reduction Factors for Early Retirement at Ages 62 and 65 for Workers and Spouses, Based on Year of Birth

(Factors for spouses apply to 50% of the worker's PIA)

First claiming benefits at age 62:

Year of Birth	Reduction Factor	
	Retired Worker	Spouse
1937 or before	20.00%	25.00%
1938	20.83	25.83
1939	21.67	26.67
1940	22.50	27.50
1941	23.33	28.33
1942	24.17	29.17
1943-54	25.00	30.00
1955	25.83	30.83
1956	26.67	31.67
1957	27.50	32.50
1958	28.33	33.33
1959	29.17	34.17
1960 or after	30.00	35.00

First claiming benefits at age 65:

Year of Birth	Reduction Factor	
	Retired Worker	Spouse
1937 or before	NONE	NONE
1938	1.11%	1.39
1939	2.22	2.78
1940	3.33	4.17
1941	4.44	5.56
1942	5.56	6.94
1943-54	6.67	8.33
1955	7.78	9.72
1956	8.89	11.11
1957	10.00	12.50
1958	11.11	13.89
1959	12.22	15.28
1960 or after	13.33	16.67

Early Retirement Reductions

If your benefit is reduced because you started it before the Full Retirement Age, the reduction is **permanent.** Your benefit does not increase to the full PIA when you reach Full Retirement Age. However, if your benefit is reduced for any month that you have more **earnings** than Social Security allows (pages 54-58), this reduction will be adjusted at the Full Retirement Age. Then, your benefit will be refigured so that the permanent reduction is no longer based on any months that your benefit was suspended, in whole or in part, because of your earnings.

Late Retirement

If you wait until after your FRA to claim your Social Security benefit, you can earn DRCs up to age 70. Your benefit will be increased by the percentage factor shown in the following table (prorated for months). This will also occur with respect to months when you completely lose benefits because of the earnings limitation (see pages 54-58). For birth years beginning in 1925, the annual percentage increase rises $\frac{1}{2}\%$ each two years until it reaches 8% for persons born in 1943 or later. The following table illustrates this important provision:

Year of Birth	Increase for Each Year That Benefits Are Delayed Beyond the Full Retirement Age (Prorated for Months)
1917-24	3.0%
1925-26	3.5%
1927-28	4.0%
1929-30	4.5%
1931-32	5.0%
1933-34	5.5%
1935-36	6.0%
1937-38	6.5%
1939-40	7.0%
1941-42	7.5%
1943 or later	8.0%

The benefit increase is prorated for partial years. For example, if you were born in 1935, the percentage increase is 6% per year or ½% for each month of delayed retirement.

When the increase becomes 8%, this will be an "actuarial equivalent," which simply means that, for persons who live to an average life expectancy, the value of the benefit at the Full Retirement Age will be the same as the value of the benefit if claimed at a later age. One effect of this will be to greatly reduce the importance of the Social Security earnings limitation (pages 54-58), because what you don't get "today" will be paid "tomorrow." The larger benefit may be needed when you are fully retired and without income from work; also, the benefit may be less likely to be fully or partially subjected to income taxes.

Earnings after the FRA may increase your AIME and, thus, your PIA. Any increase in your PIA will increase your benefits and those of family members who receive benefits based on your earnings. The delayed retirement credit affects only the benefits paid to workers, and surviving spouses, and does not increase the benefits of other family members.

Begin Social Security at 62, 65, or later?

One of the most commonly asked Social Security questions is whether retirement benefits should be started at age 62, or whether one should wait until later. People generally expect an easy "yes" or "no" answer, but unfortunately the question is not that simple. It depends on individual circumstances.

Beginning Social Security retirement benefits at the earliest permissible age of 62 as compared to the full retirement age of 65 is intended to be an "actuarial equivalent." This means that workers, on average, come out the same financially under either alternative. However, actuarial equivalents depend on the current real rate of return on invested money (i.e., after allowing for price inflation) and also on the sex and health of the individual. Consequently, the 20% reduction of benefits at age 62 is only a form of "rough justice."

The mathematics of each case and the rate of return on invested money are important considerations. Equally important, however, are factors such as the need for the income at age 62, whether much work will be performed after age 62, the sex of the individual, whether the benefit is for a worker or spouse, the condition of health, and the expected longevity.

If one is no longer employed at age 62, and the income is essential, commencing benefits then is the right decision. If significant earnings after age 62 are expected, then deferring the commencement of benefits may be desirable rather than getting into the complications of the Social Security earnings limitation (see pages 54-59). For example, if one started benefits at age 62, went back to work six months later for one year, **until age 65** he or she would still be charged the reduction factor for three years (20%) even though collecting "early" benefits for only two years (although, at age 65, the reduction factor would be reduced to the two-year one — 13⅓%).

With the growing popularity of defined contribution retirement plans (e.g., 401(k) thrift plans), retirement at age 62 might qualify one for a large lump-sum distribution. This may eliminate the cash-flow need to commence Social Security benefits early. On the other hand, deferring receipt of the distribution, or rolling it over into an Individual Retirement Account (IRA), may achieve additional tax deferred investment growth. Also, only part of the Social Security benefits are subject to income taxes, and for lower-income persons none is taxable (see pages 24-25).

Since women at age 65 have a life expectancy of about four years greater than men, a woman in good health (and not impoverished) can often "beat the odds" by deferring Social Security benefits based on her own work record until age 65.

With respect to spouse benefits, however, generally a woman should start the benefit at age 62 (if eligible), because in the event of her husband's death, she would be entitled to his larger benefit amount with no cost for having taken her spousal benefit early. Of course, "early" benefits for a wife often are a combination of her own earned benefits and those based on her husband's work — provided he has started his benefits. In this case, the portion based on her own work would be reduced permanently.

Potential benefits for a surviving spouse require other facts to be considered. For example, if a husband commenced reduced benefits before the Full Retirement Age (FRA) of 65, the "cost" will be higher if he leaves a widow with no significant work record of her own. At her FRA, she would **not** collect his full Primary Insurance Amount (PIA) but rather his reduced benefit (but not less than 82.5% of his PIA). On the other hand, at age 60, she can commence an actuarially reduced widow's benefit of 71.5% of her husband's PIA with no additional cost because her deceased husband started his benefit early. Again, health conditions must be considered before making a judgment and also the difference in ages as between the spouses.

The health and family longevity factors are important. If the insured worker lives beyond the "normal" life expectancy, then if he or she waits to receive the full benefit (primary insurance amount) at age 65, this is obviously advantageous.

For those looking for a purely analytical answer to their question, the mathematics is easy for an actuary, but not so simple for ordinary citizens. If a retired worker at age 62 invested all Social Security payments at a "real" rate of interest of $2\frac{1}{2}\%$, at age 80 he or she would have accumulated about the same amount of money as if commencement of benefits had been deferred to age 65 and the larger payments had been invested at the same rate of interest. Age 80 would be the life expectancy of a man at age 65. Taking a slightly different approach, at various assumed interest rates (e.g., 4%, 5%, and

6%), calculations could be made to determine how long one would have to live for the accumulated sums to be equal.

The fact that Social Security payments are now subject to income taxes in many cases is an added complication. While many pay nothing at all, some pay income tax on 50% of their benefits, some on 85%, and some at a combination of these rates (see pages 24-25). State laws vary.

Calculations can be made in individual cases but never with absolute certainty. Rates of return are not always guaranteed, longevity is never certain, and changes in the law may occur.

In general, eligible spouses should commence their benefit at age 62, female workers should generally defer theirs until 65, and for male workers, it's a "toss-up." The need for the money, condition of health and expected longevity are the critical factors.

Federal law prohibits separation of employees on the basis of age if they are able to satisfactorily perform their normal duties. Many persons work beyond the FRA of 65 and become eligible for Delayed Retirement Credits (DRCs). For persons attaining the FRA in 1999, the 5½% increase for each year of delayed retirement is **not** an "actuarial equivalent" (defined earlier). (It **will** be when the DRC becomes 8% per year for those born in 1943 or later.) The small difference of 2½% is relatively unimportant compared with earnings from continued work. The question of whether to retire "late" is essentially the same decision process of whether to retire "early." The key factors again are the need for the money, the condition of health and the expected longevity. One additional consideration may be that, currently, a widow(er), age 65 or over, of a worker who dies at age 65 or over would receive 100% of a deceased worker's benefits, **including the DRC amounts.** (The benefit for a retired worker's spouse, age 65 or older, is 50% of the worker's PIA and does **not** include any DRCs.)

Earnings Limitation for Employees (Retirement Test)

If you **continue to work** for an employer after your Social Security benefits start, some or all of the benefits may be suspended due to the earnings limitation. It applies until you reach age 70. The earnings limitation is a retirement test and is separate from the issue of income taxes (see page 24).

Beginning with the year that your benefits start, you can earn up to a certain amount in each year without affecting your benefits in any way. But if you earn **more** than the earnings limitation, Social Security will suspend some or all of your benefits and/or your family members' benefits based on your work record. If a family member earns more than the earnings limitation, only that person's benefit is reduced.

The 1999 earnings limitation for beneficiaries **ages 65-69** is **$15,500** (also applies to persons who reach age 70 but only for earnings before the month of reaching age 70). For beneficiaries **under age 65** it is **$9,600**. These amounts increase every year, based on changes in the average earnings of all employees in the country, except for persons ages 65-69, the law establishes the limits as $17,000 for 2000, $25,000 for 2001, and $30,000 for 2002.

If you are **under age 65,** benefits are reduced by **$1 for every $2** you earn over the earnings limitation during the year. If you are **65-69** (and for the months in the calendar year before the month of reaching age 70), the reduction is **$1 for every $3** you earn over the limitation. For example, let's assume that you are age 65 and start receiving Social Security retirement benefits in 1999. If you earn $45,500, this would be $30,000 over the permissible amount of $15,500. The loss in benefits would be $10,000 ($30,000 ÷ 3).

In the first year that there is a month in which you are entitled to benefits and do not earn more than $\frac{1}{12}$ of the annual Earnings Limit, a **monthly test** is used **if it gives you better results** than the annual test just described. During that year, beginning with your month of entitlement, you can receive your benefit for any month that you do not earn more than $\frac{1}{12}$ of the earnings limitation. If you earn more than $\frac{1}{12}$ of the annual limit, benefits are not payable for that month unless they are payable under the regular annual test.

In some cases, you might continue working and also apply for retirement benefits, especially if family members are eligible for benefits on your earnings record. The benefits will be reduced because of the excess earnings, but this may be better than no benefits at all. Each case must be studied carefully to see whether the earnings after taxes are worth the reduction in benefits. Remember, too, that Social Security benefits are often tax free, while earnings are subject to federal, state, and local income taxes, as well as Social Security and Medicare taxes.

In the calendar year in which you plan to retire, you might consider applying for benefits in January, even if you have not stopped working yet (pages 61-63). If your total earnings for the calendar year are not more than the earnings limitation, you will get benefits for all months in that year that are after the month when you reached age 62 (and, if over FRA, for some earlier months).

Earnings Limitation for Self-Employed

If you are self-employed, you also are subject to the earnings limitation until age 70. The annual limitation is the same as for employees. A special **alternative** test applies for the first year that you receive benefits and have, at the same time, a month when you do not perform substantial services in self-employment. Your work is examined to determine such months, and benefits are paid for those months. In general, fewer than 15 hours of services in a month is not considered substantial; more than 45 hours of services in a month is considered substantial. Between those guidelines, your services are considered substantial if you are in a highly skilled occupation.

For the annual earnings limitation, the profits and losses of all your businesses are added together to determine the earnings for the year. If the total profit was over the earnings limitation, your Social Security benefits will be reduced, even if some of the businesses lost money.

Earnings from self-employment received after retirement are generally counted when you receive them, rather than when earned. However, earnings from work performed before the month you become entitled to retirement benefits do not count towards the earnings limitation (except that income received in the year of retirement counts for the annual limitation).

If you are self-employed and also employed by others, you must combine your salary and wages and your net income or loss from self-employment to see whether your earnings exceed the earnings limitation.

Income for Earnings Limitation

Certain types of income are **not** counted as earnings in applying the earnings limitation. Some of these are:

- pensions and retirement pay;

- vacation or bonus pay earned in a prior year;

- 401(k) plan and IRA withdrawals;

- employee contributions pursuant to a salary reduction under a Section 125 cafeteria plan to fund a qualified benefit;

- payments from certain tax-exempt trust funds such as profit sharing, bond purchase, or annuity plans;

- severance payments made on account of retirement;

- dividends and interest from investments (unless you are in the brokerage business) and capital gains;

- rental income unless you are in the real estate business;

- non-cash payments for domestic service;

- tips not in cash or amounting to less than $20 in a month;

- sick pay if paid more than 6 months after the month last worked;

- workers' compensation and unemployment insurance benefits;

- reimbursement for travel or moving expenses to the extent they are not counted as income by the Internal Revenue Service;

- damages, fees, interest, or penalties received in a court judgment, except that back pay recovered must be counted as wages or salary; and

- contest or lottery winnings.

Even if the earnings limitation causes a loss of the entire benefit for a period of time, Medicare coverage is not affected.

You may receive some benefits retroactively for as many as six months but not for any month prior to your Full Retirement Age. (For disability benefits, the retroactive period can be as much as 12 months.) This could happen if you were eligible for benefits but did not apply on time.

Because some payments made after retirement are subject to payroll taxes (pages 19-20), Social Security may erroneously believe that you are working and subject to the earnings limitation even if you have retired. The most common situations that can cause problems involve payments for accrued vacation pay, bonuses, and nonqualified deferred compensation arrangements. In such cases, you may need your former employer to document the types of payment that were made and whether they represented compensation for current services. Generally, payments for **past** services will not cause benefit reductions under the earnings limitation. Some large employers have arranged to tell the Social Security Administration automatically about such payments to prevent the standard inquiries from being sent to their retirees.

Notify Social Security of Excess Earnings

Social Security beneficiaries who expect to earn over the allowable limit (under the rules of the annual earnings test — see pages 54-58) should notify Social Security as early as possible.

In most cases, you can provide the necessary information over the telephone by calling Social Security toll free at **800-772-1213**.

It is important to notify Social Security as soon as possible if there is a change in your estimated earnings. They will make any necessary adjustments in your benefits as new information is received.

This will enable Social Security to pay you the correct amount of benefits. If your actual earnings are less than what you estimate, then Social Security may owe you additional benefits. If your actual earnings are more than you estimate, then you may be overpaid.

Estimating your earnings is usually simple for employees. It can be more complicated for those who own or control a business. Social Security may ask more detailed questions as circumstances warrant. Social Security recognizes that such persons sometimes have opportunity to disguise their actual earnings in attempts to circumvent the rules of the annual earnings test.

Applying for Benefits

If you think you are eligible for benefits, you should file an application. It is better to apply for benefits and be denied than not to apply for benefits to which you are entitled. It's also important to apply on time, because there are strict limits on retroactive benefits. (See pages 61-63 for a detailed discussion of when to apply for retirement benefits.)

You can apply for Social Security benefits by telephone or in person at a local office. You can call Social Security at **800-772-1213** and schedule an appointment either for a telephone application or a personal interview; they will advise you what documents you need. Social Security will need original or certified copies of documents. They will make their own photocopies and return all documents to you.

Almost all applicants will need to present a birth certificate. In the rare case where a birth certificate is not available, Social Security will advise what alternative documents can be submitted. You should know your own Social Security number and the number of your spouse.

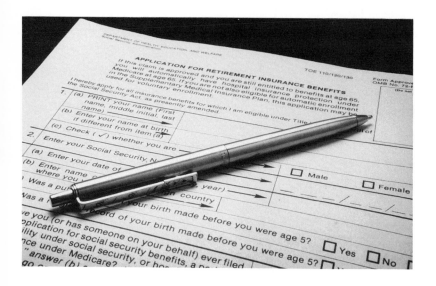

When To Make Application for Social Security Benefits

The Social Security Administration advises people to file claims up to four months before they want the benefits to begin, but it does not always recommend what month is best for the claimant's first effective month. This section will address that issue.

First, there is the question of retroactivity of benefits when they are not filed for in a timely manner. The Omnibus Budget Reconciliation Act (OBRA) of 1990 eliminated the right to file for non-disability benefits retroactively with respect to reduced benefits before FRA. In some cases, this can cause a large disparity in benefit amounts for two claims which are identical except for the application date.

For example, Mr. Anderson and Mr. Thomas (who have no eligible dependents) have both earned at least the maximum amount taxed by Social Security each year throughout their adult lives. Their Primary Insurance Amounts (PIAs), payable at age 65 in 1999, are $1,373 per month. Prior to attaining age 65 in July 1999, they had reduced their work loads some, but each had earned $32,450 to date. They both reduced their work hours further, but earn $1,300 per month for the rest of the year starting in July.

Mr. Anderson applied for Social Security retirement benefits in July, effective for that month. Because his earnings each month for the balance of the year exceed the permissible amount of $1,292 under the Social Security monthly earnings limitation, he cannot receive benefits under this test (page 54). Neither can he collect any benefits for 1999 when he uses the annual earnings test, demonstrated as follows:

Earnings, first 6 months	$32,450	
Earnings, second 6 months	7,800	(6 mos. × $1,300/mo.)
Total	$40,250	
Permissible earnings	15,500	
Excess earnings	$24,750	
Potential loss of benefits	$ 8,250	(one-third)
Benefit amount, second 6 months	$ 8,238	(6 mos. × $1,373/mo.)

Mr. Thomas on the other hand, applies for benefits in January, with the effective date that month even though he also intends to work through June. His benefit is reduced slightly from his PIA of $1,373 because of claiming it six months before the Full Retirement Age. The reduction is 3.33%, making the benefit $1,327 ($1,373 × .9667). He **cannot** use the monthly earnings test either because of exceeding the permissible earnings of $1,292 in each month of the year. He **can** use the annual earnings test to his advantage, however, as follows:

Earnings, first 6 months	$32,450	
Earnings, second 6 months	7,800	(6 mos. × $1,300/mo.)
Total	$40,250	
Permissible earnings	15,500	
Excess earnings	$24,750	
Potential loss of benefits	$ 8,250	(one-third)
Benefit (January-June)	$ 7,962	(6 mos. × $1,327/mo.)
Difference	$ 288	(benefit loss for July)

Because all benefits payable for months before attaining age 65 have been withheld, the benefit amount is recomputed and increased to the unreduced $1,373. Now, the remaining $288 of benefits to be withheld is met by paying Mr. Thomas $1,085 for July ($1,373 – $288). Combined with $6,865 (5 mos. × $1,373) for the balance of the year, his total benefits are $7,950 greater than Mr. Anderson — simply by applying earlier. If he had a wife or other family members who were entitled to benefits on his work record, the difference in benefits could be much larger. In the case of Mr. Anderson, there would be a small compensating offset for the loss of $8,238 in benefits. This would occur because a Delayed Retirement Credit (page 49) for six months (July - December) would later be payable, for life, on his benefits at a rate of 2.75% ($6/12 \times 5.5\%$).

The example stated is an extreme one and the loss of benefits by Mr. Anderson could have easily been avoided by limiting his earnings after June to $1,292 per month or less. New beneficiaries who expect to have significant earned income after retirement, however, should apply in January of the year in which they plan to commence benefits, just to be safe. However, if you plan to apply for benefits in the year in which you attain the minimum age to qualify (age 62), you cannot apply more than four months before attaining that age.

For persons who become age 66 to 69 in a particular year during which they plan to "retire," the best strategy is to file the claim effective for no later than July. Under these circumstances, full retroactivity to the start of the year would be possible. The law permits retroactivity in these cases because, in doing this, there is no reduction in benefits. Similarly, persons who attain age 70 in a particular year and are still working, should file a claim effective for at least the month of becoming 70. In any event, for persons of any age beyond 65, filing a claim effective for January would not be a disadvantage.

Family Benefits

When you retire and become entitled to Social Security benefits, other members of your family may also become entitled to benefits based on your earnings record. Their benefits are figured as a percentage of your PIA (not necessarily your **benefit**) subject to the Maximum Family Benefit. This maximum can reduce all benefits except the worker's benefit. After the application of the maximum, your **retirement** benefit will be lower than your PIA if it begins before the Full Retirement Age (FRA), and it will be larger than your PIA if you retire later. The following table shows the percentage of your PIA payable to your family members when you retire:

Who Receives Benefits When You Retire	
Benefits Paid To:	Percent of Your PIA Payable:
Spouse, age 65*	50%
Spouse, age 62	37.5%**
Spouse, any age, with eligible child who is under age 16 or disabled	50%
Each eligible child	50%
* When the FRA for workers rises, this age will rise, too. ** Gradually reduced starting in the year 2000 (pages 45 and 153).	

You must apply for benefits before your family members can become entitled to benefits on your work record (except as noted below for divorced spouses). The benefits payable to your family members are **in addition** to your benefit.

Spouse

To qualify for benefits, your spouse must have been married to you for at least one year or be the parent of your child. A spouse who first becomes entitled to benefits at or after the FRA, will receive an amount equal to 50% of your PIA. At age 62, your spouse can receive permanently reduced benefits, currently 37½% of your PIA (pages 46 and 153). You must begin your benefit before your spouse can collect a benefit on your work record.

If your spouse is also insured for a retirement benefit, that benefit will be paid, plus a spouse's benefit **limited** to the excess (if any) by which 50% of your PIA exceeds his or her own PIA. This excess is reduced if the spouse's benefit starts before the FRA. This spouse's benefit is then added to his or her own retirement benefit. This is done automatically by Social Security and is not a matter of choice.

A **spouse who is caring for your eligible child** is entitled to an amount equal to 50% of your PIA. The eligible child must be under age 16 (or any age, if disabled before age 22). In this case, no reduction is made because of the spouse's age.

Your **unmarried divorced spouse** may be entitled to benefits starting at age 62 if married to you for at least 10 years (but cannot receive benefits solely on the basis of caring for an eligible child). This benefit is not payable if your divorced spouse is remarried, unless the marriage is to a person receiving benefits as a widow, widower, parent, or disabled child. These benefits are subject to the same reductions as other spouse's benefits if they start before the Full Retirement Age. A divorced spouse can receive benefits if you are at least age 62 (whether retired or not) or are receiving Social Security disability benefits. If you are 62 but not retired, then the divorce must have been at least two years ago before your divorced spouse can receive benefits. If you were entitled to benefits before the divorce, your divorced spouse can receive benefits at once.

Eligible Child

The definition of **child** includes your natural child, adopted child, stepchild (who must be dependent on you for at least 50% support), and dependent grandchild (if the parents are deceased or disabled). An eligible child must be unmarried and:

- under age 18; or
- age 18, if in high school; or
- any age, if disabled before age 22.

Each child is entitled to 50% of the parent's PIA — based on the PIA of either parent, whichever is greater, but not both.

Maximum Family Benefit

The total amount of benefits that all members of one family may receive based on the **earnings record of one worker** is limited to an amount that varies with the PIA. The table on pages 84 and 85 shows this **Maximum Family Benefit** for various AIMEs and PIAs for persons who reach age 62 in 1999 or who become disabled or die before age 62 in 1999. (The calculation rules are on page 152.) The maximum is higher for retirement and survivor cases than for disability cases. The maximum applies before any reduction for early retirement or any increase for late retirement. **The family maximum does not apply if both a husband and wife receive only a retirement benefit based on his or her own work record.**

If the sum of the individual benefits based on your earnings record is more than the maximum, the benefits of the family members will be reduced proportionately to bring the total within the limit. Your worker's benefit will not be reduced. An example on pages 98-100 shows how this applies to survivor benefits.

The amount payable to a divorced spouse of a worker, whether or not the latter is alive, is not included in figuring the MFB, with one exception: the benefit of a surviving divorced spouse qualifying only on the basis of caring for a child of the worker **is** included in figuring the maximum.

Example — Retirement Benefits

Married Couple:	Joe	Marilyn
Born	1938	1937
Age 62 in	2000	1999
PIA	$1,000	$400*

* **Note:** Marilyn was not employed when her children were young, and stopped her employment several years before reaching age 62.

Marilyn's Benefit

At age 62, Marilyn can receive a benefit on her own earnings record. She doesn't have to wait for Joe to retire. Her PIA is $400. Because she is starting her benefit before age 65, it is reduced by $5/9$ of 1% for each month — or a reduction of 20% for 36 months. This reduces her monthly benefit to $320 at age 62. Marilyn could continue to receive this amount, plus cost-of-living increases **(applicable also in all of the following cases),** for the rest of her life. However, when Joe retires, she will receive a larger monthly benefit based partly on **his** earnings record.

Joe's Benefit

If Joe retires next year at age 62, his PIA will be $1,000. This must be reduced in the same way that Marilyn's was (20% for the three years before age 65), resulting in a monthly benefit of $800. If Joe remains retired, he'll receive this amount for the rest of his life.

If Joe claims his benefit at age 62 but continues to work and earns more than the earnings limitation, his benefit would be further reduced (pages 54-55), as would Marilyn's spouse benefit. Her benefit based on **her** work record, however, is not affected by Joe's earnings.

When Joe reaches age 65, his benefit and Marilyn's spouse benefit will be increased to recognize any months in which benefits were withheld or reduced because of his work. If he continues to work after age 65, he will receive delayed retirement credits for months when benefits are withheld completely (page 49). Also, the additional years of earnings after age 62 would probably increase his PIA above $1,000.

Marilyn's Spouse Benefit

Marilyn can collect benefits based on Joe's work record **whenever** he retires. If her wife's benefit begins at age 65, she may receive an amount up to 50% of Joe's PIA — or $500. If Marilyn had no work history under Social Security, she would receive this amount each month. However, Marilyn has earned a PIA of $400, which must be subtracted from the $500, resulting in a spouse's benefit of $100.

If she claims this benefit before age 65, it will be reduced by $25/36$ of 1% for each month. This reduction is different from the one used for her own PIA (page 47). At age 63, the reduction would be $16\frac{2}{3}\%$, or about $17, resulting in a spouse's benefit of $83. Combined with her own benefit of $320 started at age 62, she would receive $403 a month while both she and Joe are alive.

If Joe and Marilyn both wait until age 65 to receive benefits, even though he stopped working at age 62, each would receive the full PIAs they had earned — $1,000 for Joe and $400 for Marilyn. In addition, Marilyn would receive a spouse's benefit of $100, which brings her total payments to $500 — an amount equal to 50% of Joe's PIA.

If Joe had the lower earnings record, and Marilyn had the higher earnings record, the total benefit payments would be the same as in the example described.

Reduction of Benefits Because of Other Pensions

The "Windfall" Elimination Provision

A provision of Social Security law, called the **windfall elimination,** modifies the method of computing the retirement or disability (but not survivor) PIA, resulting in lower benefit amounts. This applies to many people receiving pensions based on their own earnings from employment **not covered** by Social Security. This includes some government pensions, as well as pensions from foreign employment.

The purpose of the windfall elimination provision was to close a loophole that enabled people who worked in both covered and noncovered employment to receive the unintended advantage of the weighted Social Security PIA formula. The PIA formula is weighted in favor of the career low-level earner because such a person is more dependent on Social Security for retirement income needs than higher-income people. Such persons who work in both covered and noncovered employment appear to be low earners when only their covered earnings are considered, and thus they would receive large benefits in relation to such earnings if it were not for this provision.

Exceptions are:

- persons reaching age 62 before 1986;
- persons **eligible** for such pensions before 1986;
- disabled-worker beneficiaries disabled before 1986;
- persons with at least 30 years of substantial Social Security coverage, defined as follows;
- federal employees who were mandatorily covered by Social Security on January 1, 1984; and
- persons employed on January 1, 1984, by nonprofit organizations that were not covered by Social Security at any time before 1984.

The special computation method substitutes a lower factor for the 90% ordinarily applied to the first interval of the PIA formula (page 151). Except as noted below, the factor that is substituted is 80% for workers born in 1924; 70% for workers born in 1925; 60% for workers born in 1926; 50% for workers born in 1927; and 40% for workers born in 1928 and later.

For workers with at least 21 years of substantial Social Security covered earnings, a larger factor may be applicable, as follows:

Years of Work	Special Factor		Years of Work	Special Factor
30	90%		24	60%
29	85		23	55
28	80		22	50
27	75		21	45
26	70		20 or fewer	40
25	65			

Substantial earnings for each year are:

Year	Substantial Earnings		Year	Substantial Earnings
1937-50*	$ 900		1983	$ 6,675
1951-54	900		1984	7,050
1955-58	1,050		1985	7,425
1959-65	1,200		1986	7,875
1966-67	1,650		1987	8,175
1968-71	1,950		1988	8,400
1972	2,250		1989	8,925
1973	2,700		1990	9,525
1974	3,300		1991	9,900
1975	3,525		1992	10,350
1976	3,825		1993	10,725
1977	4,125		1994	11,250
1978	4,425		1995	11,325
1979	4,725		1996	11,625
1980	5,100		1997	12,150
1981	5,550		1998	12,675
1982	6,075		1999	13,425

*Total credited earnings from 1937-50 are divided by $900 to get the number of years of coverage (maximum of 14 years).

The windfall elimination provision only modifies the PIA computation. Unlike the government-pension offset (discussed next), it cannot reduce the computed benefit to zero. Also, it does not apply to computing the PIA for survivor benefits.

Government Pension Offset (Spouses)

If **you** worked for a federal, state, or local government and were **not covered by Social Security** when your employment ended, two-thirds of your pension benefits from that employment will be offset against any Social Security benefit for which you are eligible as a **spouse, widow,** or **widower.** You can receive only the amount of the Social Security benefit that exceeds two-thirds of your government pension. This frequently eliminates Social Security benefits altogether. This reduction rule does not apply to:

- persons entitled to Social Security benefits before December 1977;

- all women (except divorced wives and widows who had fewer than 20 years of marriage to the worker), and men who were dependent on their wives, who received, or were eligible to receive, government pensions any time during December 1977 through November 1982; and

- persons eligible to receive government pensions during December 1982 through June 1983 who were dependent on their spouses.

This provision of the law is called the **government pension offset.** It is important to understand that this provision only applies to Social Security benefits that you receive as a dependent or survivor, not to benefits you earned as a worker. This offset also does not affect Medicare eligibility.

Example: Doris was a school teacher for 25 years and was never covered by Social Security. Her husband's Primary Insurance Amount is $1,000 a month. At FRA or older, she is eligible to receive an amount equal to 50% of $1,000, or $500 a month. But her teacher's pension is $900, and two-thirds of this is $600, which exceeds the $500 amount. Thus she cannot receive a Social Security benefit on her husband's work record. If her teacher's pension were $600, two-thirds (or $400) would be offset against her $500 wife's benefit under Social Security, and she could collect $100 a month.

Many retired government employees affected by the government pension offset consider that they are being singled out for unfair treatment. In fact, the purpose of the law is to treat them similarly to other retirees who worked in Social Security covered employment. The amount of any dependent or survivor benefit payable under Social Security is offset by the amount of any Social Security retirement or disability benefit that a person receives based on his or her own earnings. For instance, in the example described, if Doris had earned a PIA of $500 or more on her own Social Security work record, she could not collect a benefit based on her husband's work record.

The government pension offset can reduce the Social Security spouse or survivor benefit to zero, but not always. Even if a spouse benefit is reduced to zero, this does not necessarily mean that, later, a higher survivor benefit would also be reduced to zero. Suppose, for instance, that Doris' husband dies. She would be eligible to receive his PIA of $1,000 a month, minus an amount equal to two-thirds of her teacher's pension.

It is important to apply for benefits and let Social Security make a formal determination. Don't just assume that you aren't eligible. Also, if your benefit is reduced to zero, you can still qualify for Medicare Part A.

5 *Disability Benefits*

If you have worked long enough under Social Security and become severely disabled more than six months before attaining your Full Retirement Age (FRA), you can receive a monthly disability benefit which is equal to what your PIA was at the time that the disability occurred. The benefit is not reduced because it starts before the FRA, currently 65. However, if you become disabled after age 62 and have already received a reduced retirement benefit, your disability benefit will be reduced to take into account the number of months you received the retirement benefit.

Easy-Reference Table

The table on the next page shows the approximate benefits for you and your family if you become disabled in 1999. The figures assume that you have worked steadily and received average pay raises throughout your working career. By following the steps described on pages 78-81, you can make a more accurate calculation.

Like other Social Security benefits, disability benefits are increased each year to reflect changes in the cost of living.

A Maximum Family Benefit (page 66) applies, and this can be determined from the table on pages 84-85 by finding your PIA in column 2 and looking across to the last column. In all the examples shown below, the maximum is 150% of the benefit shown for you (which is the PIA).

Monthly Benefits at Disability

Your Age in 1999	Who Receives Benefits	Your Present Annual Earnings				
		$20,000	$30,000	$45,000	$60,000	$72,600 and Up
64*	You	$742	$977	$1,227	$1,327	$1,384
	Child or children & spouse	371	488	613	663	692
60	You	793	1,042	1,318	1,431	1,494
	Child or children & spouse	396	521	659	715	747
55	You	793	1,043	1,332	1,464	1,539
	Child or children & spouse	396	521	666	732	769
50	You	793	1,043	1,337	1,496	1,587
	Child or children & spouse	396	521	668	748	793
45	You	793	1,043	1,338	1,514	1,624
	Child or children & spouse	396	521	669	757	812
40	You	793	1,043	1,338	1,514	1,641
	Child or children & spouse	396	521	669	757	820
35	You	794	1,044	1,338	1,514	1,649
	Child or children & spouse	397	522	669	757	824
30	You	794	1,045	1,339	1,516	1,657
	Child or children & spouse	397	522	669	758	828

*Disability benefits are not paid to persons 65 or over.

Qualifications for Disability Benefits

Disability means that you are so severely impaired, physically or mentally, that you cannot perform any substantial gainful work. The impairment must be expected to last at least 12 months or to result in earlier death. The determination must be based on medical evidence and is ordinarily made by a government agency in your state. Disability benefits are not payable to persons disabled solely due to alcoholism or drug addiction.

To qualify for disability benefits, you must have earned a minimum number of credits of Social Security coverage (as defined on page 30). In addition, you must have earned some of these credits in recent years.

The following table summarizes the requirements for anyone becoming disabled in 1999. If you were born on January 1, refer to the year prior to the year of your birth.

Year of Birth	Credits Required To Qualify for Disability Benefits in 1999
1934-37	40, with 20 earned in last 10 years
1938	39, with 20 earned in last 10 years
1939	38, with 20 earned in last 10 years
1940	37, with 20 earned in last 10 years
1941	36, with 20 earned in last 10 years
1942	35, with 20 earned in last 10 years
1943	34, with 20 earned in last 10 years
1944	33, with 20 earned in last 10 years
1945	32, with 20 earned in last 10 years
1946	31, with 20 earned in last 10 years
1947	30, with 20 earned in last 10 years
1948	29, with 20 earned in last 10 years
1949	28, with 20 earned in last 10 years
1950	27, with 20 earned in last 10 years
1951	26, with 20 earned in last 10 years
1952	25, with 20 earned in last 10 years
1953	24, with 20 earned in last 10 years
1954	23, with 20 earned in last 10 years
1955	22, with 20 earned in last 10 years
1956	21, with 20 earned in last 10 years
1957-68*	20 earned in last 10 years
1969*	19 earned after age 21
1970*	17 earned after age 21
1971*	15 earned after age 21
1972*	13 earned after age 21
1973*	11 earned after age 21
1974*	9 earned after age 21
1975*	7 earned after age 21
After 1975	6 earned in last 3 years

*The figure shown is the maximum number of credits required. Depending on month of birth and month of disability, the number can be up to 3 fewer, with a minimum of 6 credits.

Waiting Period

Disability benefits begin after a waiting period of five full calendar months. To qualify for benefits, you must have been disabled throughout this period. For example, if you become disabled on January 15, you could not receive benefits for January or the next five months, February through June. The first benefit would be for July and would normally be paid in August. If you previously received disability benefits and the disability ended less than five years before the present disability began, you will not have a second waiting period.

Disability benefits can be paid retroactively for up to 12 months, not including the waiting period. If a disabled worker dies before filing a claim, the family can apply for the disability benefits within three months of the worker's death.

Family Benefits

If you become entitled to disability benefits, your eligible spouse or children can receive benefits under the same rules that would apply if you retired (page 64). The Maximum Family Benefit, including your benefit, is generally 150% of your PIA. This is lower than for retirement and survivor benefits (pages 66, 84-85 and 152).

The following table shows the percentage of your PIA payable to your family members if you qualify for disability benefits.

| Who Receives Benefits If You Become Disabled in 1999 | |
Benefits Paid To:	Percent of Your PIA Payable:
Spouse, age 65*	50%
Spouse, age 62	37.5%**
Spouse with child under age 16 or disabled	50%
Each eligible child	50%
* When the FRA for workers rises, this age will rise, too.	
** Gradually reduced starting in the year 2000 (pages 45 and 153).	

Rehabilitation

When you apply for disability benefits, you may be referred to the appropriate state agency for rehabilitation services.

Workers' Compensation

The law provides for a possible offset of disability benefits when you have been awarded workers' compensation or certain other disability benefits under federal, state, or local law. The total of all such disability benefits may not exceed 80% of your recent earnings before your disability began. Benefits from the Department of Veterans Affairs based on financial need and benefits based on government employment covered by Social Security do not cause any reduction.

Earnings Limitation

The usual earnings limitation (pages 54-58) does not apply to disabled beneficiaries. It does apply, however, to working spouses and children who receive benefits as the dependents of disabled beneficiaries.

Trial Work

If you are a disabled beneficiary, you are encouraged to go back to work, if you are able to. However, you must notify Social Security of all work attempts. Benefits can continue throughout a nine-month (not necessarily consecutive) trial work period, plus an additional three-month grace period. A month in which earnings exceed $200 generally counts as a month of trial work.

After completion of the trial work period, additional earnings are evaluated to determine if they are substantial. Earnings in excess of $500 a month generally constitute substantial gainful work. The threshold for blind beneficiaries is $1,100. After the three-month grace period, benefits are suspended if earnings are considered substantial. Benefits can be reinstated during a 36-month extended period of eligibility for any month that earnings do not exceed $500.

Medicare coverage can continue for at least 39 months after completion of the trial work period.

Anyone under 65 who continues to have a disabling impairment, and who has lost Medicare coverage after 36 months due to work, can purchase Parts A (Hospital Insurance) and B (Medical Insurance) by paying the monthly premiums (pages 106 and 111).

How To Figure Your Disability Benefit Amount

Your disability benefit equals your PIA at the time that disability occurs. To figure your PIA, you need to know your earnings history, because your PIA is based on your Average Indexed Monthly Earnings (AIME). By following the steps below, you can figure your own AIME. This, in turn, will give you a good estimate of your PIA if you become disabled in 1999. The following instructions do not apply to persons born before 1937.

How To Figure Your AIME and PIA:

(1) In column C of the worksheet on page 81, enter your earnings for each year through 1998. **You can get past information from the Earnings and Benefit Estimate Statement** that you can receive from Social Security (page 176). If your earnings for any year were more than the Maximum Taxable Amount, use the maximum only.

(2) Multiply earnings for all years by the factors in column D. These index factors make past earnings comparable to earnings today. Enter the results of your multiplication in column E, Indexed Earnings.

(3) Not all indexed earnings are used to figure your AIME. The table on the next page shows how many years of earnings to use if you become disabled in 1999. If you were born on January 1, refer to the year prior to the year of your birth. (The rule for determining how many years to use is on page 151.) If you are disabled after age 24 but before age 37, you may reduce the number of years shown by one for each year in which a child of yours (or of your spouse)

under age 3 lived in your home, and you were not employed (up to a maximum of 2 years if you are age 26-31 and of 1 year if you are age 25 or age 32-36).

Number of Years Used To Figure AIME			
Year of Birth	Number of Years	Year of Birth	Number of Years
1934-37	35	1957	16
1938	34	1958	16
1939	33	1959	15
1940	32	1960	14
1941	31	1961	13
1942	30	1962	12
1943	29	1963	12
1944	28	1964	11
1945	27	1965	10
1946	26	1966	9
1947	25	1967	8
1948	24	1968	8
1949	23	1969	7
1950	22	1970	6
1951	21	1971	5
1952	20	1972	4
1953	20	1973	4
1954	19	1974	3
1955	18	After 1974	2
1956	17		

Circle the number of years you must use.

(4)   On the worksheet, put check marks in column F by the years of your highest indexed earnings shown in column E. Continue until you have checked the number of years you must use from step 3.

(5) Add up all the indexed earnings in column E for the years you have checked in column F. ....$ _____

(6) Multiply the number of years in step 3 by 12 to get months. ... _____

(7) Divide the total earnings shown in step 5 by the months shown in step 6 to get your AIME (drop cents). ... $ _____

Now, to figure your PIA:

(8) Look at the table on pages 84-85. Find your AIME from step 7 as closely as possible in the first column of the table. The numbers on this line show your approximate PIA and the disability benefits based on it. For a more precise benefit determination, apply the 1999 benefit formula shown on page 151. The benefit amount is increased by the cost-of-living percentage effective for December each year and payable in January. A different method of computing the PIA in connection with disability benefits (producing lower amounts) applies to people receiving a pension based on their earnings from noncovered employment — see page 69.

Worksheet for Figuring Your Indexed Earnings Only if Born After 1936

A Calendar Year	B Maximum Taxable Amount	C Enter Your Taxable Earnings	×	D Index Factor	=	E Indexed Earnings	F High Years
1951	$3,600			9.79794			
1952	3,600			9.22403			
1953	3,600			8.73595			
1954	3,600			8.69111			
1955	4,200			8.30728			
1956	4,200			7.76421			
1957	4,200			7.53106			
1958	4,200			7.46529			
1959	4,800			7.11292			
1960	4,800			6.84432			
1961	4,800			6.71094			
1962	4,800			6.39092			
1963	4,800			6.23795			
1964	4,800			5.99302			
1965	4,800			5.88702			
1966	6,600			5.55367			
1967	6,600			5.26063			
1968	7,800			4.92232			
1969	7,800			4.65340			
1970	7,800			4.43339			
1971	7,800			4.22128			
1972	9,000			3.84451			
1973	10,800			3.61813			
1974	13,200			3.41512			
1975	14,100			3.17765			
1976	15,300			2.97253			
1977	16,500			2.80446			
1978	17,700			2.59814			
1979	22,900			2.38914			
1980	25,900			2.19172			
1981	29,700			1.99127			
1982	32,400			1.88737			
1983	35,700			1.79970			
1984	37,800			1.69978			
1985	39,600			1.63032			
1986	42,000			1.58332			
1987	43,800			1.48840			
1988	45,000			1.41853			
1989	48,000			1.36451			
1990	51,300			1.30426			
1991	53,400			1.25740			
1992	55,500			1.19579			
1993	57,600			1.18560			
1994	60,600			1.15461			
1995	61,200			1.11011			
1996	62,700			1.05835			
1997	65,400			1.00000			
1998	68,400			1.00000			

Note: Index factors change each year based on change in U.S. average wage.

Example — Disability Benefits

Jim and His Family

Jim is disabled at age 47 in 1999. His PIA is $1,000. He has a wife, Donna, age 47; a son, Steve, age 12; and a son, Mike, age 8.

Jim's Qualifications for Disability Benefits

When Jim became disabled, he had earned 60 credits of Social Security coverage since he was 21, including 20 in the last 10 years. He had enough credits to be eligible for benefits.

He was disabled on February 15 and had to wait five full calendar months — March through July — until his benefit began. His first payment, which was for August, came in September.

Jim is entitled to his PIA of $1,000, with no reduction because of his age, plus cost-of-living increases. Each of the three other members of Jim's family would be entitled to $500, which is an amount equal to 50% of Jim's PIA. This adds up to a total of $2,500, which is over the Maximum Family Benefit of $1,500. Jim can receive his full benefit of $1,000, but each family member receives $166. (The total is less than $1,500 due to rounding.)

Benefits Payable

Jim	$1,000
Donna	166
Steve	166
Mike	166
Total	$1,498

Jim, Two Years Later (2001)

Jim, still disabled, becomes eligible for Medicare in August 2001, even though he's far from 65 years old. Jim's family is not eligible for Medicare, however.

Six Years Later (2005)

Steve's benefit stops when he reaches age 18 and completes high school. Because the family benefit is still 150% of the PIA, the total remains the same. Jim receives $1,000, Donna receives $250, and Mike receives $250.

Eight Years Later (2007)

Social Security reviews the case periodically to see if Jim, age 55, remains disabled. His disability continues.

Jim's youngest child, Mike, is 16. Donna's benefit stops because she is no longer caring for a child under age 16.

If Mike is still in high school, his benefit of $500 can continue until age 19; otherwise, it stops at age 18.

Jim and Donna, Age 62 in 2014

At 62, Donna is again eligible for benefits as Jim's wife. She is entitled to an amount equal to 50% of Jim's PIA when she is 66, which is the Full Retirement Age for workers and spouses born in 1952. However, because she is receiving the benefit at 62, it is reduced by 30%, and she receives $350.

Jim continues to receive his PIA of $1,000 as a disability benefit. Their total income is $1,350.

Jim and Donna, Age 66 in 2018

Jim's disability benefit stops when he reaches Full Retirement Age, but his retirement benefit begins automatically. It's the same amount — $1,000.

If Donna had waited until 66 to receive her benefit, she would have been entitled to the full 50% of Jim's PIA, or $500.

Their total retirement benefit would then have been:

Jim	$1,000
Donna	500
Total retirement income	$1,500

6 *1999 Benefit Table*

Table of Monthly Social Security Benefits As To Persons Reaching Age 62, or Dying or Becoming Disabled Before Age 62, in 1999[1]

(If your exact AIME is not shown, your benefit will be between the benefits for the AIMEs just above and below your AIME.)

	Benefits for Workers and Their Families					Benefits for Survivors of Deceased Workers					
			Benefits for Family Members								
			Spouse[3] Not Caring for Child		Child or Spouse Caring for Child	Spouse[3] not Caring for Child		One Child	Spouse[3] and One Child, or Two Children	Maximum Family Benefit for Retirement and Survivors[5]	Maximum Family Benefit for Disability
Average Indexed Monthly Earnings (AIME)	Age-65 Retirement Benefit or Disability Benefit[2]	Age-62 Retirement Benefit	Age 65	Age 62		Age 65	Age 60 or Age 50-59 and Disabled				
	100% of PIA	80% of PIA	50% of PIA	37½% of PIA	50% of PIA	100% of PIA	71½% of PIA	75% of PIA	150% of PIA	150-188% of PIA	100-150% of PIA
$ 800	$ 548	$ 439	$274	$205	$274	$ 548	$ 392	$ 411	$ 822	$ 823	$680
1,000	612	490	306	229	306	612	438	459	918	919	850
1,200	676	541	338	253	338	676	483	507	1,014	1,054	1,015
1,400	740	592	370	277	370	740	529	555	1,110	1,228	1,111
1,600	804	643	402	301	402	804	575	603	1,206	1,402	1,207
1,800	868	695	434	325	434	868	621	651	1,302	1,576	1,303
2,000	932	746	466	349	466	932	667	699	1,398	1,747	1,399
2,200	996	797	498	373	498	996	712	747	1,494	1,833	1,495
2,400	1,060	848	530	397	530	1,060	758	795	1,590	1,919	1,591
2,600	1,124	899	562	421	562	1,124	804	843	1,686	2,005	1,687
2,800	1,188	951	594	445	594	1,188	850	891	1,782	2,091	1,783
3,000	1,252	1,002	626	469	626	1,252	895	939	1,878	2,192	1,879

3,200	1,290	1,032	645	483	645	1,290	922	967	1,934	2,257	1,935
3,400	1,320	1,056	660	495	660	1,320	943	990	1,980	2,310	1,980
3,600	1,350	1,080	675	506	675	1,350	965	1,012	2,024	2,362	2,025
3,800	1,380	1,104	690	517	690	1,380	986	1,035	2,070	2,415	2,070
4,000	1,410	1,128	705	528	705	1,410	1,008	1,057	2,114	2,467	2,115
4,200	1,440	1,152	720	540	720	1,440	1,029	1,080	2,160	2,520	2,160
4,463⁶	1,479	1,183	739	554	739	1,479	1,057	1,109	2,218	2,589	2,219

All numbers are rounded to the next lower whole dollar, in accordance with Social Security law. The Primary Insurance Amount (PIA) formula, the Maximum Family Benefit (MFB) formula, and the reduction factors for early retirement are shown on pages 151-153.

1   For persons who were 62 before 1999, see Item (8) on page 151. **Benefits are increased annually for changes in the cost of living in and after the first year of eligibility (e.g., becoming age 62).**

2   The disability benefit for a worker is the PIA, unless the worker was already receiving a benefit reduced for early retirement.

3   Divorced spouses who qualify receive the same benefits as spouses. Benefits for divorced spouses are not ordinarily subject to the family maximum, however.

4   A surviving spouse's benefit at age 65 is the PIA, unless the worker was receiving a benefit reduced for early retirement. In that case, the benefit will be the reduced amount that the worker was receiving, but not less than 82½% of the PIA.

5   Any reduction for retirement before age 65 for workers, spouses, and surviving spouses is deducted.

6   The maximum AIME for persons reaching age 62 in 1999 is generally $4,463, resulting in an age-62 benefit of $1,183 and an age-65 benefit of $1,479, assuming no earnings at ages 62-64. (For persons reaching age 65 in 1999, the maximum AIME is $3,926; a different table is used to obtain the monthly benefit amounts, and the maximum age-65 benefit is $1,373. See table on page 27.)

Note: Under some circumstances (generally, for younger, highly paid workers), persons who become disabled or die before age 62 can have AIMEs higher than $4,463. For example, at the extreme, a worker dying at age 29 or under in 1999 can have an AIME as high as $5,904 and a PIA of $1,701.

The amount of the benefits payable to your survivors is based on your PIA on the date of your death.

Easy-Reference Table

The table on the next page shows the approximate monthly benefit amounts payable to your family members if you die in 1999. The figures are based on the assumption that you have worked steadily and received average pay raises throughout your working career. By following the steps described on pages 94-97, you can make a more accurate calculation.

Like other Social Security benefits, survivor benefits are increased each year to reflect changes in the cost of living.

Monthly Benefits if You Die in 1999

Your Age in 1999	Who Receives Benefits	$20,000	$30,000	$45,000	$60,000	$72,600 and Up
		Your Present Annual Earnings				
65	Spouse at FRA*	$736	$969	$1,216	$1,316	$1,373
	Spouse at age 60	526	693	869	941	981
	Child; spouse caring for child	552	727	912	987	1,029
	Family maximum	1,277	1,757	2,127	2,302	2,401
60	Spouse at FRA*	793	1,042	1,318	1,431	1,494
	Spouse at age 60	566	745	942	1,023	1,068
	Child; spouse caring for child	594	782	989	1,073	1,121
	Family maximum	1,370	1,895	2,307	2,504	2,616
55	Spouse at FRA*	793	1,043	1,332	1,464	1,539
	Spouse at age 60	566	745	952	1,047	1,100
	Child; spouse caring for child	594	782	999	1,098	1,154
	Family maximum	1,370	1,895	2,331	2,563	2,694
50	Spouse at FRA*	793	1,043	1,337	1,496	1,587
	Spouse at age 60	566	745	956	1,069	1,135
	Child; spouse caring for child	594	782	1,003	1,122	1,190
	Family maximum	1,370	1,895	2,341	2,618	2,778
40	Spouse at FRA*	793	1,044	1,338	1,514	1,645
	Spouse at age 60	567	746	957	1,082	1,176
	Child; spouse caring for child	595	783	1,003	1,135	1,233
	Family maximum	1,371	1,897	2,342	2,650	2,879
30	Spouse at FRA*	797	1,050	1,342	1,520	1,671
	Spouse at age 60	570	750	960	1,087	1,194
	Child; spouse caring for child	598	787	1,007	1,140	1,253
	Family maximum	1,383	1,905	2,350	2,660	2,924

*FRA (Full Retirement Age) ranging from age 65 to age 67, see notes on page 44.

Lump-Sum Death Benefit

When you die, whether still working or retired, a lump sum of $255 is payable to a surviving spouse who was living with you at the time of death. If you don't have a spouse living with you, then payment may be made to a spouse or children who are immediately eligible for monthly benefits based on your earnings record. Otherwise, the benefit is not payable.

Qualifications for Survivor Benefits

For your survivors to receive monthly benefits or the lump-sum death payment, you must be either:

- currently insured (provides eligibility for some benefits, but not all), or
- fully insured (provides eligibility for all benefits).

Currently Insured

To be currently insured, you need to have earned six credits during the 13 calendar quarters ending with the calendar quarter in which you die.

If you are **currently insured,** the lump-sum death benefit is payable, and the following survivors qualify for monthly benefits:

- a spouse or divorced spouse caring for an eligible child who is under age 16 or disabled before age 22, and
- any eligible children under age 18; or age 18, if in high school; or disabled before age 22.

Fully Insured

The following table shows how many credits you need to be **fully insured.** To use the table, find your year of birth. Next to it is the number of credits you must have if you die in 1999. For example, if you were born in 1940, you need 37 credits to be fully insured. If you were born on January 1, refer to the year prior to the year of your birth. (The rule for determining the number of credits required is on page 151.)

Credits Required To Be Fully Insured if You Die in 1999

Year of Birth	Credits	Year of Birth	Credits
1929-37	40	1955	22
1938	39	1956	21
1939	38	1957	20
1940	37	1958	19
1941	36	1959	18
1942	35	1960	17
1943	34	1961	16
1944	33	1962	15
1945	32	1963	14
1946	31	1964	13
1947	30	1965	12
1948	29	1966	11
1949	28	1967	10
1950	27	1968	9
1951	26	1969	8
1952	25	1970	7
1953	24	After 1970	6
1954	23		

Family Benefits

The following table shows some examples of surviving family members who may receive benefits based on your PIA. The table also shows the percentage of your PIA ordinarily payable to each member.

Who Receives Benefits if You Die in 1999	
Benefits Paid To:	**Percent of Your PIA Payable:**
Spouse, age 65*	100%
Spouse, age 62	82.9%**
Spouse, age 60	71.5%
Disabled spouse, age 50-59	71.5%
Spouse under age 61 with eligible child who is under 16 or disabled	75%
Each eligible child	75%

 * When Full Retirement Age for workers rises (page 44), this age will rise too (but starting two years later); also, see following discussion if you receive reduced retirement benefits.
** Slightly reduced, starting in 2002 (pages 45 and 153).

Eligibility

Your spouse qualifies for survivor benefits if:

- married to you for at least nine months before your death (if death is due to an accident or military duty, no length of marriage is required), or

- the parent of your child (natural or adopted).

Surviving Spouse, Age 60 or Over

If you die before you are entitled to retirement benefits, or after retiring at the Full Retirement Age (FRA), the benefit is 100% of your PIA if your spouse has reached FRA. If your spouse is younger, a reduction applies (page 153).

For a **surviving spouse's benefit,** the reduction factor applied to the Primary Insurance Amount of the deceased worker when the Full Retirement Age (FRA) is 65 is $^{19}/_{40}$ of 1% for each month that commencement is prior to the surviving spouse's FRA — to a maximum reduction of 28.5%. (The FRA is slightly different from that for workers and spouses — for example, age 67 for those born in 1962, or later (as compared with age 67 being the applicable age for workers and spouses born in 1960, or later). If the FRA is greater than 65, the benefit will be reduced by 28.5% prorated for the number of months that commencement of payment precedes the FRA as compared with the number of months between age 60 and the FRA. For example, if the FRA is 67, and the age when benefits are claimed is $63^1/_2$, then benefits precede the FRA by 42 months ($3^1/_2$ years). This is one-half of the 84-month (7-year) period between age 60 and 67. Accordingly, the reduction is one-half of the 28.5% or 14.25%.

If you retired before the FRA and had a reduced benefit, your spouse will receive the **smaller** of:

- the amount of your PIA, with a reduction applied if your spouse is under the FRA at time of entitlement or

- the reduced benefit that you were receiving (but in no case less than $82^1/_2$% of your PIA).

If you retired after the FRA, your spouse will receive the same benefit (including the delayed retirement credit) that you had, but reduced if your spouse is under the FRA at the time of entitlement.

Your **divorced spouse** qualifies for a benefit if married to you for at least 10 years. The benefit is the same as that payable to a spouse.

If your surviving spouse or surviving divorced spouse remarries before age 60, benefits are not payable unless (and until) the subsequent marriage ends. Remarriage after attaining age 60 does not prevent or stop entitlement to benefits.

Disabled Surviving Spouse

Your **disabled spouse** age 50-59 who meets the definition of disability (see page 74) will qualify for benefits if the disability has lasted five full months. The benefit is 71½% of your PIA.

Your **disabled divorced spouse** qualifies in the same way as a disabled spouse if you were married at least 10 years.

Remarriage by your disabled surviving spouse or disabled surviving divorced spouse after age 50 and after the date he or she became disabled, does not affect entitlement to benefits.

Surviving Spouse Caring for Child

Your **spouse or divorced spouse caring for an eligible child** who is under age 16, or disabled before age 22, receives 75% of your PIA. The benefit stops when the youngest child reaches age 16, unless caring for an eligible child who was disabled before age 22. Your divorced spouse is not required to have been married to you for a specified length of time for this type of benefit. Remarriage terminates the benefit of the surviving spouse (but not the child's benefit).

Eligible Child

An eligible child (page 66), qualifies for a benefit of 75% of the deceased parent's PIA. If both parents are deceased, a child can qualify for benefits on the earnings record of either the mother or father, whichever gives the larger benefit. If the child gets married, the benefit usually terminates.

Dependent Parents

Your mother or father age 62 or over can qualify for survivor benefits if, at the time of your death, he or she was receiving at least one-half support from you. The benefit is 82½% of your PIA. However, if both parents are entitled to benefits, each receives 75%.

Maximum Family Benefit

The Maximum Family Benefit described on page 66 applies.

Non-Duplication of Benefits

A person eligible for more than one Social Security benefit for a particular month receives, in effect, the larger of the two benefits. For example, a widow of a deceased worker may receive a retirement benefit based on her own work record or a widow's benefit, but not both amounts.

Earnings Limitation

Anyone receiving survivor benefits (except on account of disability) is subject to the earnings limitation applicable to those receiving retirement benefits and will lose benefits if earnings exceed the limit. This is especially applicable in the case of employed young widows with eligible children. (Note: special rules apply to survivors entitled on the basis of disability — pages 64-66.) If a family member earns more than the limitation, this does not reduce the benefits of the other family members, and in some cases will not even reduce the total family benefits. See pages 54-58 for a full explanation of this limitation.

Spouse Government Pension Offset

Surviving spouses who are entitled to a government pension based on employment not covered by Social Security may have their survivor benefit offset (page 71).

How To Figure Survivor Benefits

Survivor benefits are based on your PIA at the time of your death. To figure your PIA, you need to know your earnings history, because your PIA is based on your Average Indexed Monthly Earnings (AIME). By following the steps below, you can figure your own AIME. This, in turn, will give you a good estimate of your PIA if you die in 1999. The following instructions do not apply to persons born before 1937.

How To Figure Your AIME and PIA:

(1) In column C of the worksheet on page 97, enter your earnings for each year, including 1999. **You can get past information from the Earnings and Benefit Estimate Statement** that you can receive from the Social Security Administration (page 176). If your earnings for any year were more than the Maximum Taxable Amount, use the maximum only.

(2) Multiply earnings for all years by the factors in column D. These index factors make past earnings comparable to earnings today. Enter the results of your multiplication in column E, Indexed Earnings.

(3) Not all indexed earnings are used to figure your AIME. The table on the next page shows how many years of earnings to use for death in 1999. If you were born on January 1, refer to the year prior to the year of your birth. (The rule for determining the number of years to use is on page 151.)

Number of Years Used To Figure AIME			
Year of Birth	Number of Years	Year of Birth	Number of Years
1929-37	35	1954	18
1938	34	1955	17
1939	33	1956	16
1940	32	1957	15
1941	31	1958	14
1942	30	1959	13
1943	29	1960	12
1944	28	1961	11
1945	27	1962	10
1946	26	1963	9
1947	25	1964	8
1948	24	1965	7
1949	23	1966	6
1950	22	1967	5
1951	21	1968	4
1952	20	1969	3
1953	19	After 1969	2

Circle the number of years you must use.

(4)   On the worksheet, put check marks in column F by the years of your highest indexed earnings shown in column E. Continue until you have checked the number of years you must use from step 3.

(5) Add up all the indexed earnings in column E for the years you have checked in column F. . . . $ _____

(6) Multiply the number of years in step 3 by 12 to get months. . . . _____

(7) Divide the total earnings shown in step 5 by the months shown in step 6 to get your AIME (drop cents) . . . . $ _____

Now, to figure your PIA:

(8) Look at the table on pages 84-85. Find your AIME from step 7 as closely as possible in the first column of the table. The numbers on this line are your approximate PIA and the survivor benefits based on it. For a more precise benefit determination, apply the 1999 benefit formula shown on page 151. The benefit amount is increased by the cost-of-living percentage effective for December each year and payable in January.

Worksheet for Figuring Your Indexed Earnings Only if Born After 1936

A Calendar Year	B Maximum Taxable Amount	C Enter Your Taxable Earnings	×	D Index Factor	=	E Indexed Earnings	F High Years
1951	$3,600			9.79794			
1952	3,600			9.22403			
1953	3,600			8.73595			
1954	3,600			8.69111			
1955	4,200			8.30728			
1956	4,200			7.76421			
1957	4,200			7.53106			
1958	4,200			7.46529			
1959	4,800			7.11292			
1960	4,800			6.84432			
1961	4,800			6.71094			
1962	4,800			6.39092			
1963	4,800			6.23795			
1964	4,800			5.99302			
1965	4,800			5.88702			
1966	6,600			5.55367			
1967	6,600			5.26063			
1968	7,800			4.92232			
1969	7,800			4.65340			
1970	7,800			4.43339			
1971	7,800			4.22128			
1972	9,000			3.84451			
1973	10,800			3.61813			
1974	13,200			3.41512			
1975	14,100			3.17765			
1976	15,300			2.97253			
1977	16,500			2.80446			
1978	17,700			2.59814			
1979	22,900			2.38914			
1980	25,900			2.19172			
1981	29,700			1.99127			
1982	32,400			1.88737			
1983	35,700			1.79970			
1984	37,800			1.69978			
1985	39,600			1.63032			
1986	42,000			1.58332			
1987	43,800			1.48840			
1988	45,000			1.41853			
1989	48,000			1.36451			
1990	51,300			1.30426			
1991	53,400			1.25740			
1992	55,500			1.19579			
1993	57,600			1.18560			
1994	60,600			1.15461			
1995	61,200			1.11011			
1996	62,700			1.05835			
1997	65,400			1.00000			
1998	68,400			1.00000			
1999	72,600			1.00000			

Note: Index factors change each year based on U.S. average wage.

Example — Survivor Benefits

In 1999, John dies at age 45, leaving four survivors. Each family member is entitled to a monthly benefit based on John's PIA of $1,000, as shown below:

Survivor	Qualification for Benefit	Percent of John's PIA	Unadjusted Monthly Benefit Amounts
Mary	Wife, age 45, caring for child under age 16	75	$ 750
Bob	Age 18, in high school	75	750
Suzanne	Age 15	75	750
Bruce	Age 11	75	750
		Total	$3,000

In the case of John's family, the Maximum Family Benefit is $1,837 (see table on pages 84-85). This means that everyone's benefit must be reduced proportionately so that the total doesn't go over that amount.

Adjusted Monthly Benefit Amounts

Mary	$ 459
Bob	459
Suzanne	459
Bruce	459
Total	$1,836

Bob Graduates from High School

When Bob graduates from high school at age 18, he is no longer eligible for Social Security benefits. His monthly benefit of $459 stops. However, the rest of the family continues to receive the same total benefit. From the total original entitlement of $3,000, subtract $750 for Bob, leaving $2,250. That's still larger than the Maximum Family Benefit of $1,837. The total stays the same, but each person's benefit will now be for a different amount.

Readjusted Benefits after Bob Graduates

Mary	$ 612
Suzanne	612
Bruce	612
Total	$1,836

Bruce Reaches Age 16

Mary's benefit as a mother caring for an eligible child stops when Bruce reaches age 16. (Suzanne is ineligible by then because she is over age 18.) However, Bruce remains entitled to his benefit of $750 until he is 18 (or until 19 if he is still in high school).

Bruce Reaches Age 18

When the youngest child reaches age 18 and has completed high school, all the children's benefits will have stopped. No further benefits are payable until Mary reaches age 60, unless she becomes disabled and qualifies as a disabled surviving spouse.

Mary at Age 60 in 2014

Mary can claim a surviving spouse's benefit of $715 a month for the rest of her life. That amount is 71½% of John's PIA of $1,000. Or, she can wait until she reaches her Full Retirement Age of 66 to start receiving her benefit which will then be $1,000 per month. If she works after her benefits begin, she is subject to the earnings limitation (pages 54-58).

Mary at Age 66 in 2020

If Mary waits until she is 66 before receiving benefits, she will receive 100% of John's PIA, or $1,000 a month. The earnings limitation continues to apply until age 70.

8 *Medicare*

Introduction

Are You Missing Out?

Social Security and Medicare will pay about $625 billion in benefits in 1999, most of it tax-free. About $232 billion of the total is for Medicare benefits, **all** of which is tax-free.

This section of the book explains in simple, practical terms what you need to know about Medicare. It includes a description of both the **Original Medicare Plan** and the new **Medicare+Choice** options. Also explained are:

- the 10 standard **Medigap** plans
- **taxes and premiums** you pay
- when you get your **coverage**
- how to **make sure** you get it.

Medicare could pay many of your medical expenses, if you know what to do and when to do it. Don't miss out. Read this booklet!

What is Medicare?

Medicare is the federal health insurance program for persons age 65 and over and certain disabled persons. It consists of Part A (Hospital Insurance) and Part B (Medical Insurance). Once you are eligible for Part A and are enrolled in Part B, you can choose either to stay in the Original Medicare Plan, or else enroll in a Medicare+Choice plan (if one is available in your area).

The **Original Medicare Plan** is a traditional indemnity or fee-for-service plan. Most Medicare beneficiaries are in the Original Medicare Plan.

Legislation in 1997 created additional options, available in 1999, known as **Medicare+Choice** plans. Such health plans include several types of managed care. Persons who choose to enroll in a Medicare+Choice plan opt to receive healthcare services through such a health plan instead of the Original Medicare Plan. It is expected that a growing number of beneficiaries will be in Medicare+Choice plans in the future.

Who is Eligible for Medicare?

Part A (Hospital Insurance)

You are eligible for Medicare Part A Hospital Insurance if you are **age 65 or over** and are eligible for any type of monthly Social Security benefit. It is available on the first day of the month you attain age 65. You establish your entitlement with the Social Security Administration. Your application can be retroactive for up to six months. Such eligibility can be for benefits as a retired worker, as a spouse of a retired or disabled worker, or as a surviving spouse of a deceased worker. Even if you are not eligible in one of the ways described, you and your spouse can be eligible on the basis of your government employment on which you paid the Medicare payroll tax. There is no eligibility for people who receive monthly benefits solely on the basis of one of the international agreements on Social Security that the U.S. has with some countries.

You qualify even if you do not receive monthly Social Security benefits because you or your spouse continues to work.

If you are **disabled,** you may be eligible for Medicare before age 65. You must have been entitled to disability benefits from Social Security for two years as a worker, surviving spouse, or adult child of a retired, disabled or deceased worker. You don't have to apply for a Medicare card in this event; enrollment in such cases is automatic.

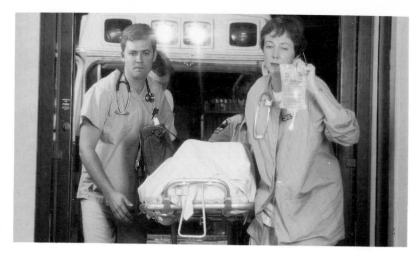

Family members of disabled workers are not eligible for Medicare benefits before age 65 unless they have been entitled to monthly benefits because of their own disability for at least two years.

Special provisions apply to persons with **end-stage renal disease** (kidney failure) who require dialysis or a transplant. In such cases, you are eligible for Part A at any age if you are an insured worker or the spouse or dependent child of an insured worker (including survivors of a deceased insured worker). The social service staff at the hospital or dialysis center where you receive treatment will usually assist you in applying for this coverage.

What Do You Pay for Part A (Hospital Insurance)?

Some of the payroll taxes that employees and employers pay are for Medicare Hospital Insurance. Certain government employees who are not under Social Security pay the Medicare tax and receive credits toward Part A benefit coverage. Included are federal employees hired before 1984 and state and local government employees hired after March 1986. The tax is paid on all annual earnings at a rate of 1.45%. The employer pays a matching tax. Self-employed persons pay twice this rate — 2.90%. No premiums are required for this insurance if you have sufficient Social Security credits. Almost all Medicare beneficiaries qualify for premium-free Part A.

Special rules apply to uninsured persons who are at least age 65 but not eligible for premium-free Part A under the regular rules. Uninsured persons can purchase Part A coverage by paying substantial premiums. In 1999, the standard Part A monthly premium for uninsured persons, who are not otherwise eligible for premium-free Part A, is $309. This is reduced to $170 for uninsured persons who have at least 30 credits (and their spouses). They must also enroll in Part B and pay a monthly premium for that coverage (page 107). Disabled persons who lose their cash benefits because they returned to work can continue under premium-free Part A for up to 36 months. After that time, they can purchase Medicare in the same way as uninsured persons age 65 or over.

Part B (Medical Insurance)

When you enroll in Part A of Medicare, you also automatically enroll in Part B, unless you tell the Social Security Administration that you don't want it. This procedure applies to persons age 65 or older, long-term disabled beneficiaries, and persons with kidney failure. Nearly everyone in the U.S. who is eligible for Part B will want to enroll when first eligible, unless they have primary coverage based on current employment under an employer-sponsored plan. Even if you are not eligible for premium-free Part A, you can almost always enroll in Part B at age 65. If you elect Part A on a premium basis, you must also enroll in Part B (page 105). A general enrollment period (January through March each year, with entitlement effective the following July 1) is available for persons who did not elect Part B when first eligible. A special enrollment period is available for persons who had coverage under an employer-sponsored health plan based on active employment (page 107).

What Do You Pay for Part B (Medical Insurance)?

If you enroll in Part B at the earliest opportunity, you pay premiums of **$45.50** per month during 1999. These premiums are deducted from your Social Security benefits, if you get them. Otherwise, the government bills you quarterly in advance. (Premiums from beneficiaries pay about one-fourth of the cost of the program; the balance is financed from the general revenues of the federal government.) If you enroll late, or if you drop out and enroll again, you may have to pay higher premiums. You will pay 10% more for each full 12 months that you were eligible but did not participate. You don't include in such 12-month periods any months when you weren't enrolled in Part B while covered by an employer-sponsored group insurance plan (page 123) based on your, or your spouse's, current employment. Coverage under Part B can begin when your group coverage ends. You get a special eight-month enrollment period beginning after the month when coverage ends, or when current employment status ends.

Examples of Part B Monthly Premiums

Mr. Allen took early-retirement benefits under Social Security when he reached age 63 in May 1997. On May 1, 1999, the beginning of the month he turns 65, he is automatically covered by Medicare Part A and Part B. Part A coverage was earned while Mr. Allen was working; no monthly premiums are required. Monthly premiums are required for Part B coverage, but he can refuse it if he does not want to pay the premiums. If he takes no action, the monthly premiums for Part B will be automatically deducted from his Social Security benefits, beginning with the benefit payable in May.

Ms. Evans was working and had substantial wages when she turned age 65 in 1999. She informed the Social Security Administration that she wanted to enroll in Medicare Parts A and B. The government bills her for the Part B coverage. She could have applied for only Part A if she did not want to pay the Part B premiums. When she retires and begins to receive monthly Social Security benefits, the monthly premiums will be automatically deducted from her benefits.

Mr. Garcia retired at age 65 in March 1996 and began receiving Social Security benefits. He decided not to enroll in Part B then because he believed that he was in excellent health and saw no reason to pay the premiums. Later, he decides that coverage would be desirable — especially because he would be paying far less than the value of the Part B protection. He can enroll during the first three months of 1999, with coverage beginning July 1. At that time, he will have been eligible for, but not participating in, Part B for more than three years but less than four years. Therefore, his monthly premium will be 30% higher than the standard rate for the rest of his life, or $59.20 in 1999.

Medicare as Secondary Payer

If you are eligible for Medicare benefits at age 65 or older and are working for an employer with 20 or more employees, then you are entitled to the same employer-sponsored healthcare benefits offered to younger employees. If you have such benefits and are working, then Medicare is the secondary payer, paying only with respect to charges not covered by your employer-provided plan. These rules apply to your spouse at age 65 or older if you are working for such an employer, regardless of your age if your spouse has coverage based on your current employment.

These rules also apply to disabled Medicare beneficiaries who are under age 65 and are covered by an employer-provided healthcare plan as a currently working employee or as a family member of an employee. However, this applies only if the plan is that of an employer with 100 or more employees.

In those cases where the "employer size" condition is not met, Medicare is primary, and the employer plan is secondary.

Medicare is also secondary payer for 30 months for persons who have group health insurance and have Medicare because of end-stage renal disease (kidney failure).

Under any of these circumstances, you may choose not to participate in Part B and thus not pay premiums. Or you may choose not to participate in the employer-provided plan, and have Medicare coverage only. However, in such a case, the employer cannot offer insurance to supplement Medicare, but can only provide coverage for services not covered by Medicare.

Medicare is also the secondary payer if medical costs can be paid under any liability policy, such as auto insurance.

See page 123 for an example of how Medicare pays under Part A when it is the secondary payer.

Original Medicare Plan

What Benefits Does Part A (Hospital Insurance) Provide?

In addition to the basic benefits for inpatient hospital care, Part A provides benefits for skilled nursing facility care, home health services, and hospice care. In most cases, you pay part of the costs of covered services. Most people have additional supplemental insurance from either a retiree medical plan or a private Medigap policy (pages 126-137) to cover some of the costs that Medicare doesn't cover. Medicare covers only services that are medically necessary, and it limits the charges to certain allowable amounts.

The amounts that you and/or your insurance pay change each year, depending on national increases in hospital costs. The following description is based on **1999 amounts,** which are likely to increase again the next year.

Hospital Benefits. When you are admitted to a hospital, you will have to pay an initial deductible of $768, but no more than the actual charges. After the first 60 days, you will have to pay $192 per day. After 90 days, you can choose to pay up to $384 per day for as many as 60 "lifetime reserve" days (instead of paying what the hospital charges). Your "benefit period" ends 60 days after discharge from a hospital or skilled nursing facility. If another hospital admission occurs after that, you will have to pay another deductible, as well as the coinsurance (cost-sharing) amounts described above. Appliances such as pacemakers and artificial limbs that are permanently installed while in the hospital are covered without further cost sharing.

Skilled Nursing Facility Benefits. You may qualify for limited benefits at a skilled nursing facility if both the facility and your diagnosis and treatment plan meet Medicare's strict standards. Daily skilled nursing or rehabilitation services must be available to you. Skilled nursing facility benefits are available to you only following a hospital stay of at least three days and beginning within 30 days of leaving the hospital. Medicare does not cover custodial care if that is the only care you need.

If you qualify, you pay nothing for the first 20 days, except for any charges that Medicare does not allow. For the next 80 days, you pay charges up to $96 per day, and Medicare pays all remaining allowable charges. No benefits are available after 100 days of care in a "benefit period."

Home Health Services Benefits. Home health services, such as part-time or intermittent skilled nursing care, physical therapy, medical social services, medical supplies, and some rehabilitation equipment, may be paid for in full by Medicare when you are confined at home, if the services are prescribed by a doctor. Even if you only have just Part A or Part B, all covered services will be paid by Medicare if provided by a home health agency that participates in Medicare.

Care in Psychiatric Hospitals. Part A will pay for up to 190 days of inpatient psychiatric care in a lifetime. Restrictions apply to people who are hospitalized for psychiatric care when they are first covered by Medicare (a 150-day maximum).

Hospice Benefits. A hospice is an organization that furnishes a coordinated program of inpatient, outpatient, and home care for terminally ill patients. Emphasis is on pain reduction, control of symptoms, and counseling, but not curative treatment. When you are an inpatient in a facility, in order to provide respite for your usual caretaker (not to exceed five consecutive days), you pay about $5 per day. Also, you pay 5% of the cost for prescription drugs, but not more than $5 for each prescription, for symptom management and pain relief. Hospice benefits are limited to 210 days unless you are recertified as terminally ill. When you choose hospice benefits, all other Medicare benefits stop, except for physician services and treatment of conditions not related to the terminal illness.

Care in Christian Science Sanatoriums. Part A of Medicare can help pay for inpatient hospital and skilled nursing facility services that you receive in a Christian Science sanatorium operated or listed and certified by the First Church of Christ Scientist in Boston.

Care in Non-Participating Hospitals. A few qualified hospitals do not participate in the Medicare program. Medicare will pay part or, in some cases, all of your expenses in a non-participating hospital if you have an emergency, and it's the closest hospital.

Blood Deductible. Part A will pay for inpatient blood transfusions, except for the first three pints per year. You cannot be charged for the first three pints of blood that you replace, or if the blood is part of the deductible under Part B.

Diagnosis Related Groups (DRGs)
To avoid excessive hospital stays, Medicare pays fixed amounts to hospitals for inpatient care, according to diagnosis. But your doctor still decides when you are ready to be discharged.

What Benefits Does Part B (Medical Insurance) Provide?

You or your insurance pay the first $100 of charges **allowable** by Medicare for covered medical services provided to you in a calendar year. This is the annual deductible. After that, you or your insurance will pay 20% of covered expenses (which may not exceed the charges allowed by Medicare) plus any additional amount that the physician is **allowed** to charge (page 119). The Medicare program covers only services that are medically necessary.

The annual deductible of $100 and the 20% patient coinsurance charge do not apply to certain payments (page 115).

Covered items include:

- physician services, regardless of where provided, and supplies furnished as part of such services;
- physical therapy, speech pathology, and occupational therapy by physicians or institutional providers, including outpatient rehabilitation facilities;
- services of independent physical therapists and occupational therapists, but with limits (page 116);
- non-routine vision services by qualified optometrists if they would be covered when performed by a physician;
- diagnostic x-ray, laboratory, and other tests;
- x-ray, radium, and radioactive-isotope therapy (including technician services);
- annual mammography screening at ages 40 and over;
- pap smears, colorectal screening tests and bone mass measurements;
- blood for transfusions, after the first three pints per year;
- flu shots and pneumococcal vaccine;

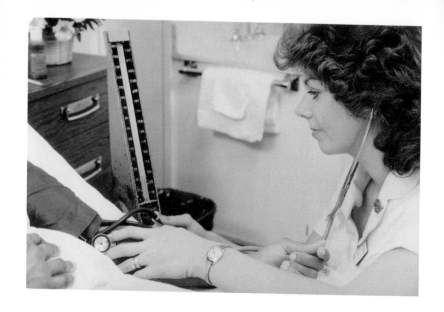

- drugs that cannot be self-administered, blood-clotting factors for hemophilia, certain oral anti-cancer drugs, injectable osteoporosis drugs, and immunosuppressive drugs used in the first year after organ transplant;

- surgical dressings, splints, casts, and similar medical supplies ordered by a doctor;

- necessary ambulance services;

- home health services;

- artificial replacements for parts of the body (covered by Part A under some circumstances);

- diabetes self-management training;

- rental of durable medical equipment used in the home, including oxygen tanks, hospital beds, and wheelchairs (sometimes, purchase of such equipment);

- ostomy bags and supplies; and

- braces for limbs, back, or neck.

Here are some special provisions:
Services Covered with No Cost-Sharing. You do not have to pay the $100 deductible or the 20% coinsurance for:

- pneumococcal vaccine and flu shots and the charge for giving them;

- outpatient clinical diagnostic laboratory tests (e.g., blood and urine tests — but not x-rays) performed by physicians (who must take assignment for such tests), by independent laboratories that are Medicare-certified, by certified hospitals (except in Maryland, where 20% coinsurance is applicable), and by rural health clinics;

- home health services;

- mammography screening, pap smears, colorectal screening tests, bone mass measurement procedures, and diabetes self-management training. These are **not** subject to the annual deductible, but **are** subject to the 20% coinsurance.

Part B helps to pay for only one type of treatment by licensed and Medicare-certified **chiropractors:** manual manipulation of the spine to correct a subluxation (vertebrae out of place) that can be demonstrated by x-ray (after 1999, the x-ray requirement is eliminated). Medicare does not pay for the x-ray or for any other diagnostic or therapeutic services furnished by chiropractors.

Outpatient treatment of **mental illness** is covered under special payment rules. You will ordinarily pay 50% of allowable charges. However, you will pay only 20% of allowable outpatient hospital charges if you would have required admission to the hospital without the treatment. Also, you will pay any additional amount that the physician is **allowed** to charge (page 119).

Part B does not usually pay for routine foot care, such as hygienic care, treatment for flat feet or other structural misalignment, or removal of calluses, corns, and most warts. It will help to pay for other services of a podiatrist, including routine care and therapeutic shoes, if the patient has a condition affecting the lower limbs such as severe diabetes.

Services of **independent physical therapists** and **occupational therapists** are covered. Medicare pays up to a maximum of $1,200 per year (80% of the maximum allowable charges of $1,500) for each type.

People who elect **hospice** benefits have certain restrictions — and also extra benefits (page 112).

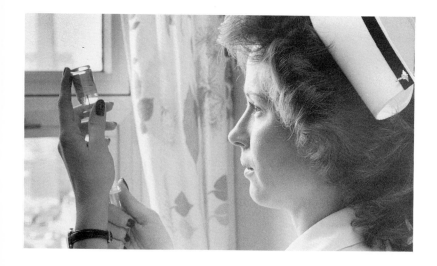

Other Provisions

What the Original Medicare Plan Does Not Cover

Medicare does not cover all healthcare expenses. A telephone call to the carrier that handles your Medicare claim is the best way to get answers to your questions about specific cases. Some of the items not covered are:

- most prescription drugs and medicines taken at home;
- services not reasonable or medically necessary;
- items or services for which you are not legally obligated to pay;
- services paid for by the government or workers' compensation;
- services performed by a relative or household member;
- services outside the U.S. (exceptions are qualified Canadian and Mexican facilities if they are nearest to your home, or if for emergency care while you are traveling to or from Alaska through Canada);
- routine physical exams;
- routine eye exams and glasses;
- hearing aids;
- dental services (except surgery on, or reduction of, any fracture of the jaw or facial bones);
- routine foot care and orthopedic shoes, except for diabetics (page 116);
- most chiropractic services (page 115);
- custodial care;
- cosmetic surgery (except after an accident);
- acupuncture;
- most immunizations (page 114);
- first three pints of blood for transfusions (each year);

- meals delivered to your home;

- private nurses;

- extra charges for a private room (unless medically necessary), telephone, television, and other personal comfort items;

- homemaker services (except under hospice provisions);

- certain services for employees and their family members who have primary coverage under employer-provided health plans (page 123);

- certain services in the first 30 months of treatment for chronic kidney disease when covered by employer-provided insurance; and

- services covered by liability or auto insurance.

Claim Number

When you become eligible for Medicare benefits, you will receive a Medicare card containing your claim number. This number is very important to keep because no claim will be paid without it. The card is the only evidence that you are covered by Medicare.

How Claims Are Paid

Claims are processed by a "fiscal intermediary" (Part A) or a "carrier" (Part B). These are insurance companies or other organizations, such as Blue Cross/Blue Shield, under contract to the government. Check your last Medicare Summary Notice or Explanation of Medicare Benefits for the name and address of the carrier. Also, the Social Security Administration (1-800-772-1213) or the Health Care Financing Administration (1-800-638-6833) can give you the name of the carrier that will process your claims. Hospital charges to be paid by Medicare are billed by the hospital to the intermediary that pays them.

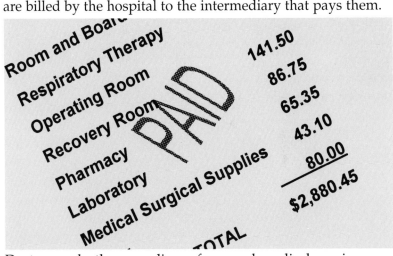

Doctors and other suppliers of covered medical services may submit charges directly to the Medicare carrier by "taking an assignment." Your doctor will receive the portion of the bill paid by Medicare and will bill you only for any part of your $100 annual deductible not already met and the 20% coinsurance payment. Doctors and suppliers who take assignments may not charge more than the amount allowable by Medicare.

Even if the doctor does not take assignment, he or she must send the claim to the Medicare carrier for you. Medicare will pay you on the portion of the bill that is allowable, and you will have to pay the doctor directly. Some charges may be higher than those allowable by Medicare, but the doctor cannot charge more than 15% above the allowable charge. Because your benefit payment will be based on the allowable charge, you will have to pay the excess over the allowable charge, any unmet part of the $100 annual deductible, and the 20% coinsurance.

Example of Medicare Benefits for Physician Visits

Mr. Allen, age 72, has acute arthritis and visits his physician, Dr. Williams, every two months for continued observation of his condition and for review of the effect of the drugs that he is taking. Dr. Williams is a "participating physician" (one who always takes assignment) and sends the bills to the Medicare carrier that handles Part B claims. Dr. Williams usually charges $47 for office visits, plus varying amounts for tests made by an outside laboratory. Medicare allows only $40 for the office visits, and so Dr. Williams can charge only this amount. Medicare pays the entire allowed amount of the laboratory-test bills. This amount is not necessarily what the laboratory would charge a non-Medicare patient, but is a rate set by Medicare.

Mr. Allen pays Dr. Williams $80 for the first two visits in 1999. The Medicare carrier allows all of this amount and applies it to Mr. Allen's annual deductible of $100. After Dr. Williams submits a $40 bill for Mr. Allen's third visit in the year, the Medicare carrier sends Mr. Allen a statement showing that the total allowable charges for the year are $120, so that the $100 deductible is met. The carrier also sends Dr. Williams a check for $16, which is 80% of $20 ($120 minus $100). Mr. Allen is responsible for paying Dr. Williams the remainder of the allowable charges of $120 directly. For subsequent visits, Medicare pays a benefit of $32 (80% of $40) to Dr. Williams, and Mr. Allen must pay him the remaining $8.

The laboratory bills Medicare directly, and Mr. Allen receives only a notice of the payments made for the services rendered.

If Dr. Williams **did not** always accept assignment, the situation would be quite different. For non-participating physicians, Medicare's allowable charges are 5% lower than for participating physicians. Thus, under these circumstances, the allowable charge for each visit would be $38 (95% of $40). Dr. Williams cannot bill Mr. Allen for more than $43.70 (115% of $38), even though his usual charge is $47. He would, as required by law, send the bills to the Medicare carrier and would bill Mr. Allen what Medicare will allow — $43.70 for each visit. After the first three visits in 1999, Medicare would tell Mr. Allen that the deductible was met, because the total allowable charges then amounted to $114, and would send him a check for $11.20 (80% of: $114 minus the $100 deductible). For each subsequent visit, Medicare would pay Mr. Allen $30.40 (80% of $38). At the same time, Mr. Allen would pay Dr. Williams $43.70 for each visit.

If Dr. Williams made the laboratory tests himself, instead of sending them to an independent laboratory, the reimbursement procedure would depend on whether he takes assignments for such tests, regardless of whether he takes assignments for other services. If he takes assignments for the tests, he would submit the bill to the Medicare carrier and receive the full allowable charge from Medicare, in accordance with a Medicare schedule, and not his usual charge. Mr. Allen would pay nothing. However, if Dr. Williams did not take assignments for such tests, Medicare would not pay anything.

Example of Medicare as Secondary Payer under Part A

For hospital bills under Part A, Medicare pays the **smaller** of (1) what would have been paid if Medicare were primary, or (2) the Medicare-allowable charge, minus what the other plan actually pays. Consider a patient who has not previously met the Part A deductible and is hospitalized in 1999, with billed charges of $2,000 and a Medicare-allowable charge of $1,600. The other plan, which has a $100 deductible and 20% coinsurance, pays $1,520 (80% of: $2,000 minus $100). If Medicare were primary, it would pay the hospital $832 ($1,600, minus the $768 deductible). Thus, the second alternative, which is smaller, is the amount paid to the hospital: $80 ($1,600, minus the $1,520 benefit under the plan).

If the other plan provided a benefit of $1,600 or more, then Medicare would pay nothing. But if it paid less than $768, then Medicare would pay $832 to the hospital (the allowable charge, minus the deductible), and the patient would pay the difference between the $768 deductible and the other plan's benefit.

In summary, the hospital always receives (from the plan, Medicare, and/or the patient) at least as much as the Medicare-allowable charge. The hospital receives more **only** when the other plan's benefit **alone** is more. The patient will usually pay nothing or, at most, only part of the Part A deductible. Even when the individual has no liability, the deductible is met for any subsequent hospitalization in that "benefit period."

Medicare Primary/Secondary Rules as Related To Employer-Provided Health Benefits[1]
(For employees of firms with 20 or more employees)

Category of Individual	Individual	Non-employed Spouse 65 or Over[2]	Spouse Under 65	Disabled Child[3]
I. Employee age 65 or over	Medicare is secondary[4]	Medicare is secondary[4,5]	No Medicare[7,9]	Medicare is secondary[4,5,9]
II. Employee age 62-64	No Medicare[6]	Medicare is secondary[4,5]	No Medicare[7,9]	Medicare is secondary[4,5,9]
III. Employee under age 62	No Medicare[6]	No Part A Medicare unless on own work record or voluntarily purchased, and Part B only if purchased; Medicare coverage when having Part A on own work record, whether or not having Part B, is secondary[4,10]	No Medicare[7,9]	No Medicare[7,9]
IV. Retiree age 65 or over	Medicare is primary	Medicare is primary	No Medicare[7]	Medicare is primary
V. Retiree age 62-64	No Medicare[7,8]	Medicare is primary	No Medicare[7]	Medicare is primary
VI. Retiree under age 62	No Medicare[7,8]	No Part A Medicare unless (a) based on own work record, (b) voluntarily purchased, or (c) the retired spouse receives Social Security disability benefits; Part B only if purchased; Medicare is primary	No Medicare[7]	No Part A Medicare unless the retired parent receives Social Security disability benefits; Part B only if purchased; Medicare is primary[8]

1   Assumes that individuals always file for Part A (Hospital Insurance), if eligible. For both employees and spouses, if Medicare Part B (Supplementary Medical Insurance) is waived because of good coverage of employer plan and to avoid paying the premiums ($45.50 per month in 1999), then such plan is primary. When employment ends (or, if earlier, when coverage under employer plan is ended or, for the disabled, when such plan is no longer primary to Medicare), the individual is eligible for a special enrollment period, and the Medicare Part B premium surcharge for delayed enrollment is waived. (Such surcharge waiver applies even though the employer has fewer than 20 employees, in which case Medicare is always primary.)

2   If spouse is aged 65 or over and is employed and covered under own employer's plan (with 20 or more employees), Medicare is secondary in any event (subject to footnote 4).

3   Receiving disabled-child benefits (based on becoming disabled before age 22) for at least 24 months after attainment of age 18, and not employed (if employed, and covered under own employer's plan subject to footnote 8; Medicare is secondary in any event — subject to footnote 4). The attendance of the disabled child at high school at age 18 (and before age 19) does not affect the running of such 24-month period.

4   Unless employer plan is waived.

5   Assumes that worker is eligible for retirement benefits (even though not receiving them because of earned income level).

6   Unless disabled and in a rehabilitation trial work period (and also in the following three months and in a further 36 months if engaging in substantial gainful employment even though not medically recovered) and meets (or had met) conditions of footnotes 7 and 8.

7   Unless, on basis of own work record, Social Security disability benefits are being received and have been received for 24 months or more.

8   For plans covering employees of at least one employer with 100 or more employees, Medicare is secondary for a disabled employee who qualifies for Social Security disability benefits and has received such payments for 24 months, but only if the disabled employee is considered to be a currently working employee; otherwise for such disabled former employees, Medicare is primary.

9   For plans covering employees of at least one employer with 100 or more employees, Medicare is secondary for the disabled spouse or child of an employee if such person, on the basis of his or her own work record, qualifies for Social Security disability benefits and has received such payments for 24 months, providing that the spouse or child is covered under the employer plan as a dependent of the employee.

10 If has only Part B, or if has Part A voluntarily purchased (and, therefore, must have Part B), then Medicare is primary.

Medicare Supplemental Insurance

The Original Medicare Plan doesn't pay all of a beneficiary's medical expenses. There are deductibles, coinsurance amounts, nonallowable charges, and noncovered services. Most people need additional health insurance to fill the gaps in the Original Medicare Plan.

Some retired persons and their spouses have adequate protection through a retiree medical plan provided by their former employer or union. Many others purchase Medicare supplement insurance, called **Medigap** policies.

Medigap policies are limited to ten standard plans (except in Massachusetts, Minnesota and Wisconsin), designated A through J, plus two high deductible plans based on Plans F and J. One basic package of benefits (Plan A) must be offered in all Medigap plans. Plans B through J offer various features in addition to the basic plan. You do not need more than one Medigap policy.

Not every insurer offers all plans. Also, premiums can vary considerably from one company to another and from area to area.

You have a 6-month open enrollment period from the date you are both enrolled in Medicare Part B and are age 65 or older. During this open enrollment period, you have the right to purchase any Medigap policy sold in your state. The company cannot discriminate in the pricing of the policy because of your health condition. All Medigap policies are guaranteed renewable.

Within the 10 standard plans, there is another option called **Medicare Select.** This is a Medigap policy with a preferred provider arrangement that has lower premiums if the participant agrees to use the services of particular healthcare providers.

More detailed information on Medigap plans is available from the respective state insurance commissioners. For general information or for the telephone number of your state insurance office, you can call the Medicare hotline at **1-800-638-6833.**

The purpose of the 1990 (effective in 1992) legislation is to standardize the coverage provided by Medicare supplement insurance, to simplify the terms, to eliminate misleading and confusing provisions, and to increase the consumer's understanding of and ability to compare them. The premium cost and, of course, service can vary among the various insurers.

This legislation applies to policies held to be, or marketed as, Medicare Supplement policies. It does not apply to employer or labor union policies for employees or members or for former employees or members.

There are several **key provisions** regarding Medigap **policies.**

- No policy can contain benefits that duplicate Medicare benefits.

- You have a six-month open enrollment period from the date you are both enrolled in Medicare Part B and are age 65 or older.

- No policy can exclude or limit benefits for loss incurred more than six months from the effective date of coverage because it involved a pre-existing condition.

- Such policies can provide that benefits which are designed to cover deductibles and coinsurance under Medicare will change automatically as they change under Medicare. Premiums, of course, may be adjusted to correspond with such changes.

- States must establish very strict guidelines regarding nonrenewability and cancellation of policies. Generally, policies are not to be canceled or nonrenewed other than for non-payment of premium.

- Applicants have the right to return a policy within 30 days of its delivery and receive a refund of the premium if not satisfied for any reason.

The **basic benefits** included in **all standard Medigap plans** are:

- Coverage of Part A Medicare coinsurance for hospitalization from the 61st day through the 90th day in any Medicare benefit period. This cost is $192 per day in 1999 (page 110);

- Coverage of Part A Medicare eligible expenses incurred for hospitalization to the extent not covered by Medicare for each Medicare lifetime inpatient reserve day used. This cost is $384 per day in 1999 (page 110);

- Upon exhaustion of the Medicare Part A hospital inpatient coverage, including the lifetime reserve days, coverage of the Medicare Part A eligible expenses for hospitalization, subject to a lifetime maximum benefit of an additional 365 days;

- Coverage under Medicare Parts A and B for the reasonable cost of the first three pints of blood (or equivalent quantities of packed red blood cells, as defined under federal regulations) unless replaced in accordance with federal regulations (page 112);

- Coverage for the coinsurance amount (20%) of Medicare Part B regardless of hospital confinement, subject to the Medicare Part B deductible of $100 (page 113).

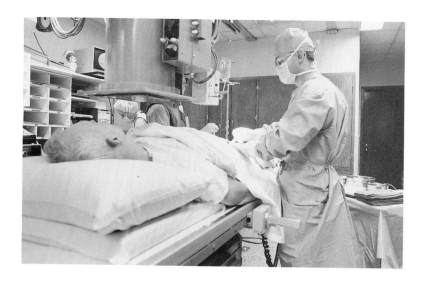

The first Medicare supplement plan, which is designated as Plan A, contains only the basic benefits listed previously.

Each of the remaining plans contains the basic benefits plus one or more of the following additional benefits:

(1) Medicare Part A Deductible: Coverage for the Medicare Part A inpatient hospital deductible amount per benefit period, which is $768 in 1999 (page 110).

(2) Skilled Nursing Facility Care: Coverage for the charges approved by Medicare up to the coinsurance amount (charges up to $96 per day in 1999) from the 21st day through the 100th day in a Medicare benefit period for post-hospital skilled nursing facility care eligible under Medicare Part A (page 111).

(3) Medicare Part B Deductible: Coverage for the Medicare Part B deductible of $100 per calendar year, regardless of hospital confinement (page 113).

(4) 80% of the Medicare Part B Excess Charges: Coverage for 80% of the difference between the actual charge as billed (not to exceed any charge limitation established by the Medicare program or state law), and the Medicare allowable Part B charge. (For federal law limits on physician charges for Medicare patients, see page 119.)

(5) 100% of the Medicare Part B Excess Charges: Coverage for all of the difference between the actual charge as billed, (not to exceed any charge limitation established by the Medicare program or state law), and the Medicare-approved Part B charge. (For federal law limits on physician charges for Medicare patients, see page 119.)

(6) Basic Outpatient Prescription Drug Benefit: Coverage for 50% of outpatient prescription drug charges, after a $250 calendar year deductible, to a maximum of $1,250 in benefits received by the insured per calendar year, to the extent not covered by Medicare (page 114).

(7) Extended Outpatient Prescription Drug Benefit: Coverage for 50% of outpatient prescription drug charges, after a $250 calendar year deductible to a maximum of $3,000 in benefits received by the insured per calendar year, to the extent not covered by Medicare (page 114).

(8) Medically Necessary Emergency Care in a Foreign Country: Coverage to the extent not covered by Medicare for 80% of the billed charges for Medicare-eligible expenses for medically necessary emergency hospital, physician,and other medical care received in a foreign country,which care would have been covered by Medicare if provided in the United States, and which care began during the first 60 consecutive days of each trip outside the United States, subject to a calendar year deductible of $250 and a lifetime maximum benefit of $50,000. For such purposes, "emergency care" means care needed immediately because of an injury or an illness of sudden and unexpected onset.

(9) Preventive Medical Care Benefit: Coverage for the following preventive health services:

   (a)   An annual clinical preventive medical history and physical examination that may include tests and services described in the next paragraph and patient education to address preventive health care measures.

(b) Any one or a combination of the following preventive screening tests or preventive services, as often as medically appropriate (if not already covered by Medicare):

  (1) fecal occult blood test and/or digital rectal examination;

  (2) mammogram;

  (3) dipstick urinalysis for hematuria, bacteriuria, and proteinauria;

  (4) pure tone (air only) hearing screening test, administered or ordered by a physician;

  (5) serum cholesterol screening (every 5 years);

  (6) thyroid function test; and

  (7) diabetes screening.

(c) Tetanus and diphtheria booster (every 10 years).

(d) Any other tests or preventive measures determined appropriate by the attending physician.

Reimbursement shall be for the actual charges up to 100% of the Medicare-approved amount for each service, as if Medicare were to cover the service as identified in Current Procedural Terminology codes of the American Medical Association, to a maximum of $120 annually for all of the services described above.

(10) At-Home Recovery Benefit: Coverage for services to provide short term, at-home assistance with activities of daily living for those recovering from an illness, injury or surgery.

    (a) For purposes of this benefit, the following definitions apply:

        (1) "Activities of daily living" include bathing, dressing, personal hygiene, transferring, eating, ambulating, assistance with drugs that are normally self-administered, and changing bandages or other dressings.

        (2) "Care provider" means a duly qualified or licensed home health aide/homemaker, personal care aide, or nurse provided through a licensed home health care agency or referred by licensed referral agency or licensed nurses registry.

        (3) "Home" shall mean any place used by the insured as a place of residence, provided that such place would qualify as a residence for home health care services covered by Medicare. A hospital or skilled nursing facility shall not be considered the insured's place of residence.

        (4) "At-home recovery visit" means the period of a visit required to provide at home recovery care, without limit on the duration of the visit, except that each consecutive 4 hours in a 24-hour period of services provided by a care provider is counted as one visit.

(b)	Coverage Requirements and Limitations:

(1)	At-home recovery services provided must be primarily services which assist in activities of daily living.

(2)	The insured's attending physician must certify that the specific type and frequency of at-home recovery services are necessary because of a condition for which a home care plan of treatment was approved by Medicare.

(3)	Coverage is limited to:

(i)	no more than the number and type of at-home recovery visits certified as necessary by the insured's attending physician. The total number of at-home recovery visits shall not exceed the number of Medicare-approved home health care visits under a Medicare-approved home care plan of treatment;

(ii)	the actual charges for each visit, up to a maximum reimbursement of $40 per visit;

(iii)	$1,600 per calendar year;

(iv)	seven visits in any week;

(v)	care furnished on a visiting basis in the insured's home;

(vi)	services provided by a care provider, as defined;

(vii)	at-home recovery visits while the insured is covered under the policy or certificate which are not otherwise excluded; and

       (viii)   at-home recovery visits received during the period that the insured is receiving Medicare-approved home care services or no more than 8 weeks after the service date of the last Medicare-approved home health care visit.

(c)   Coverage is excluded for:

    (1)   home care visits paid for by Medicare or other government programs; and

    (2)   care provided by family members, unpaid volunteers, or providers who are not "care providers," as defined.

(11) High Deductible Policy: Beneficiary is responsible for payment of all expenses up to the amount of the deductible ($1,500 in 1998-99, increased in future years by the percentage increase in the CPI(U) from the 12-month period ending with the second preceding August to such period ending with the preceding August).

(12) New or Innovative Benefits: An insurer may, with the prior approval of the state commissioner of insurance, offer policies or certificates with new or innovative benefits in addition to the benefits provided in a policy or certificate that otherwise complies with the applicable standards. Such new or innovative benefits may include benefits that are appropriate to Medicare supplement insurance and are new or innovative, not otherwise available, cost-effective, and offered in a manner which is consistent with the goal of simplification of Medicare supplement policies.

The basic benefits included in every Medigap plan are:

- Part A coinsurance;
- coverage for 365 additional hospital days after Medicare benefits end;
- Part B coinsurance; and
- the first three pints of blood each year.

This chart shows the features of the standard plans.

Standard Medigap Plans

	A	B	C	D	E	F	G	H	I	J
Basic Benefits	✓	✓	✓	✓	✓	✓	✓	✓	✓	✓
Skilled Nursing Coinsurance			✓	✓	✓	✓	✓	✓	✓	✓
Part A Deductible		✓	✓	✓	✓	✓	✓	✓	✓	✓
Part B Deductible			✓			✓				✓
Part B: Percent of Excess Actual Charge over Allowable Charge						100% ✓	80% ✓		100% ✓	100% ✓
Foreign Travel			✓	✓	✓	✓	✓	✓	✓	✓
At-Home Recovery				✓			✓		✓	✓
Basic Drugs ($1,250 limit)								✓	✓	
Extended Drugs ($3,000 limit)										✓
Preventive Care					✓					✓

Note: There are also two additional high-deductible ($1,500 out-of-pocket expenses) plans based on plans F and J.

Medicare+Choice

Introduction

Beginning in 1999, Medicare beneficiaries may opt to enroll in one of a variety of Medicare+Choice plans instead of the Original Medicare Plan. When you enroll in Medicare, you will automatically be in the Original Medicare Plan unless you elect to enroll in a Medicare+Choice plan. You must be enrolled in Medicare Parts A and B and pay the Part B monthly premium to be eligible to enroll in a Medicare+Choice plan. Also, you cannot enroll in most Medicare+Choice plans if you have end-stage renal disease (kidney failure).

In 1999, there is a continuous open enrollment period during which Medicare beneficiaries can shift from the Original Medicare Plan to a Medicare+Choice plan, or vice versa, or between Medicare+Choice plans.

Types of Plans

Medicare+Choice plans permitted under the law include: several types of managed care plans, Medical Savings Accounts, Private Fee-For-Service plans, and Religious Fraternal Beneficiary plans.

The availability, costs, and benefit provisions of different Medicare+Choice plans will vary among plans, and also depending on where you live.

Managed Care Plans

A Medicare+Choice managed care plan is a Medicare approved network of doctors, hospitals, and other health care providers that agrees to give care in return for a set monthly payment from Medicare. Beneficiaries in managed care plans may be restricted as to which doctors and hospitals they can use. Managed care plans that participate in Medicare cover all the services covered by the Original Medicare Plan, and some cover additional services such as prescription medication. Some plans may charge a premium for additional covered services. A Medicare managed care plan can reduce your out-of-pocket expenses for deductibles and copayments. Specific costs to beneficiaries vary from plan to plan. If you are enrolled in a Medicare managed care plan, you do not need Medigap insurance. However, if you later decide to disenroll from the managed care plan, you may not be able to get Medigap insurance at affordable rates.

There are several types of Medicare+Choice managed care plans.

Health Maintenance Organizations (HMOs). HMOs (established by insurance companies and other organizations) require that you use doctors and hospitals in the plan's network. Some HMOs offer a **Point of Service (POS)** option that allows you to use doctors and hospitals outside of the network for an additional fee.

Preferred Provider Organizations (PPOs). PPOs (established by insurance companies and other organizations) encourage you to use doctors and hospitals in the plan network, but all of them offer a POS option for an additional fee.

Provider Sponsored Organizations (PSOs). PSOs are managed care plans organized by groups of doctors and hospitals (rather than by insurance companies and other organizations).

Other Plans

In addition to managed care plans, the Medicare+Choice provision allows **Private Fee-for-Service (PFFS)** plans, a test program for a limited number of **Medical Savings Accounts (MSAs),** and **Religious Fraternal Beneficiary (RFB) plans.**

PFFS plans. This plan, rather than Medicare, decides how much to pay for covered services. Providers may bill you more than the plan pays (but not more than 15% extra). Also, it is very likely that you will pay a premium to the plan.

MSAs. Under an MSA plan, you purchase an insurance policy with a high annual deductible. Medicare pays the premium for the MSA plan and deposits money into a separate Medicare MSA that you establish. You can accumulate money in the MSA and use it to pay for medical costs not met by the insurance policy. There are no limits on what providers can charge you.

RFB plans. These plans may be offered by religious fraternal benefit societies for members only. No additional information is available at the time of publication.

For More Information

You can request detailed information about the Medicare+Choice plans available in your area by calling the automated **Medicare Special Information** number **1-800-318-2596,** contacting the Medicare information internet website (www.medicare.gov), or by calling your state health insurance assistance office.

Medicare Part B Carriers and State Insurance Counseling Offices (printed in plum) Telephone Numbers

The toll-free or 800 numbers listed below can be used only in the states where the carriers are located.

ALABAMA

Blue Cross/Blue Shield of Alabama

1-800-292-8855
  205-988-2244
1-800-243-5463

ALASKA

Blue Cross/Blue Shield of North Dakota

1-800-444-4606
1-800-478-6065

ARIZONA

Blue Cross/Blue Shield of North Dakota

1-800-444-4606
1-800-432-4040

ARKANSAS

Blue Cross/Blue Shield

1-800-482-5525
  501-378-2320
1-800-852-5494

CALIFORNIA

Counties of: Los Angeles, Orange, San Diego, Ventura, Imperial, San Luis Obispo, and Santa Barbara

Transamerica Occidental Life Insurance Company

1-800-675-2266
  213-748-2311
1-800-434-0222

Rest of State

National Heritage Insurance Co.

1-800-952-8627
  916-743-1583
1-800-434-0222

COLORADO

Blue Shield of North Dakota

1-800-332-6681
  303-831-2661
1-800-544-9181

CONNECTICUT

United HealthCare Inc.

1-800-982-6819
  203-237-8592 (In the Meridan
                        area)
1-800-994-9422

DELAWARE

Medicare Customer Service Center

1-800-444-4606

DISTRICT OF COLUMBIA

Medicare Customer Service Center

1-800-444-4606

FLORIDA

Blue Cross/Blue Shield of Florida

1-800-333-7586
1-800-963-5337

GEORGIA

Cahaba

1-800-727-0827
  912-927-0934
1-800-669-8387

HAWAII

Blue Cross/Blue Shield of North Dakota

1-800-444-4606
  808-586-7299

IDAHO

CIGNA

1-800-627-2782
  615-244-5650
1-800-247-4422 S.W.
1-800-488-5725

ILLINOIS

Wisconsin Physicians Services

1-800-642-6930
  312-938-8000
1-800-535-6152 TDD
1-800-548-9034

INDIANA

AdminaStar Federal

1-800-622-4792
  317-842-4151
1-800-452-4800

IOWA

Blue Cross/Blue Shield of North Dakota

1-800-532-1285
  515-245-4785
1-800-351-4664

KANSAS

Blue Cross/Blue Shield of Kansas

1-800-432-3531
  785-291-4000 (in Topeka)
1-800-432-0216 (out of state)
1-800-860-5260

KENTUCKY

AdminaStar of Kentucky

1-800-999-7608
  502-425-6759
1-800-372-2973

LOUISIANA

Arkansas Blue Cross & Blue Shield, Inc.

1-800-462-9666
   504-927-3490
      (In Baton Rouge)
1-800-259-5301

MAINE

National Heritage Insurance

1-800-492-0919
   781-741-5258
1-800-750-5353

MARYLAND

Medicare Customer Service Center

1-800-444-4606
1-800-243-3425

MASSACHUSETTS

National Heritage Insurance Company

1-800-882-1228
   781-741-5256
1-800-882-2003

MICHIGAN

Wisconsin Physicians Services

1-800-482-4045
1-800-803-7174

MINNESOTA

United HealthCare Insurance Company

1-800-352-2762
   612-884-7171
1-800-333-2433

MISSISSIPPI

United HealthCare Insurance Company

1-800-682-5417
   601-956-0372
1-800-948-3090

MISSOURI

Counties of: Andrew, Atchison, Bates, Benton, Buchanan, Caldwell, Carroll, Cass, Clay, Clinton, Daviess, DeKalb, Gentry, Grundy, Harrison, Henry, Holt, Jackson, Johnson, Lafayette, Livingston, Mercer, Nodaway, Pettis, Platte, Ray, St. Clair, Saline, Vernon, and Worth

Blue Cross/Blue Shield of Kansas

1-800-892-5900
   816-561-0900

Rest of State

Arkansas Blue Cross/Blue Shield

1-800-392-3070
   314-843-8880
1-800-390-3330

MONTANA

Blue Cross/Blue Shield of Montana

1-800-332-6146
   406-444-8350
1-800-332-2272

NEBRASKA

Blue Cross/Blue Shield of Kansas

1-800-633-1113
   402-471-2201

NEVADA

Blue Cross/Blue Shield of North Dakota

1-800-444-4606
1-800-307-4444

NEW HAMPSHIRE

National Heritage Insurance Company

1-800-447-1142
   781-741-5256
1-800-852-3388

NEW JERSEY

Xact Medicare Services

1-800-462-9306
1-800-792-8820

NEW MEXICO

Arkansas Blue Cross/Blue Shield

1-800-423-2925
   505-872-2551
1-800-432-2080

NEW YORK

Counties of: Bronx, Brooklyn, Columbia, Delaware, Dutchess, Greene, Manhattan, Nassau, Orange, Putnam, Richmond, Rockland, Suffolk, Sullivan, Ulster, and Westchester

Empire Blue Cross and Blue Shield

1-800-442-8430

County of: Queens

Group Health Insurance

212-721-1770

Rest of State

BC/BS of Western New York

1-800-252-6550
1-800-333-4114
   212-869-3850 in New York City

NORTH CAROLINA

CIGNA

1-800-672-3071
  336-665-0348
1-800-443-9354

NORTH DAKOTA

Blue Shield of North Dakota

1-800-332-6681 or
1-800-247-2267
  701-277-2363
1-800-247-0560

OHIO

Nationwide Mutual Insurance
Company

1-800-282-0530
  614-249-7157
1-800-686-1578

OKLAHOMA

Arkansas Blue Cross/Blue
Shield

1-800-522-9079
  405-848-7711
1-800-763-2828

OREGON

Blue Cross/Blue Shield of North
Dakota

1-800-444-4606
1-800-722-4134

PENNSYLVANIA

Xact Medicare Services

1-800-382-1274
1-800-783-7067

RHODE ISLAND

Blue Cross/Blue Shield of
Rhode Island

1-800-662-5170
  401-861-2273
1-800-322-2880

SOUTH CAROLINA

Blue Cross/Blue Shield of South
Carolina

1-800-868-2522
  803-788-3882
1-800-868-9095

SOUTH DAKOTA

Blue Cross/Blue Shield of North
Dakota

1-800-437-4762
1-800-822-8804

TENNESSEE

CIGNA

1-800-342-8900
  615-244-5650
1-800-525-2816

TEXAS

Blue Cross/Blue Shield of Texas

1-800-442-2620
1-800-252-9240

UTAH

Blue Cross/Blue Shield of Utah

1-800-426-3477
  801-333-2430
1-800-439-3806

VERMONT

National Heritage Insurance Company

1-800-447-1142
781-741-5256
1-800-642-5119

VIRGINIA

Counties of: Arlington and Fairfax

Medicare Customer Service Center

1-800-444-4606

Rest of State

United HealthCare

1-800-552-3423
504-985-3931
1-800-552-3402

WASHINGTON

Blue Cross/Blue Shield of North Dakota

1-800-447-4606
1-800-397-4422

WEST VIRGINIA

Nationwide Mutual Insurance Company

1-800-848-0106
614-249-7157
1-800-642-9004

WISCONSIN

WPS

1-800-944-0051
608-221-3330
1-800-828-2837 TTY/TDD
1-800-242-1060

WYOMING

Blue Cross & Blue Shield of North Dakota

1-800-422-2371
307-632-9381
1-800-856-4398

AMERICAN SAMOA

Blue Cross/Blue Shield of North Dakota

1-800-444-4606
808-586-7299

GUAM

Blue Cross/Blue Shield of North Dakota

1-800-444-4606
808-586-7299

NORTHERN MARIANA ISLANDS

Blue Cross/Blue Shield of North Dakota

1-800-444-4606
808-586-7299

PUERTO RICO/VIRGIN ISLANDS

Triple-S, Inc.

1-800-981-7015
(In Puerto Rico)
787-749-4900 (In San Juan Metro Area)

1-800-474-7448 (Virgin Islands)
787-721-8590 (Puerto Rico)
809-778-6311 (Virgin Islands)

9 *Medicaid*

Medicaid is a joint federal and state medical assistance program for persons and families with low incomes and resources. Medicaid was created in 1965 — the same year that Medicare was created. Although the words Medicare and Medicaid sound similar and are often confused with each other, they identify separate programs.

Medicare (pages 101-125) is a federal health insurance program for persons age 65 and over, persons who have been entitled to Social Security disability insurance benefits for at least 24 months, and most persons with kidney failure. Eligibility is closely related to eligibility for Social Security benefits rather than demonstrated financial need.

Medicaid is a means-tested medical assistance program. It is jointly funded by the federal and state governments. The states administer their own Medicaid programs under federal guidelines. Each state sets its own eligibility requirements, scope of covered medical services, and rates of payments. States can require some Medicaid recipients (but not those who are also Medicare beneficiaries) to enroll in managed care plans.

Persons eligible for Medicaid include recipients of Aid to Families with Dependent Children (AFDC), most persons receiving Supplemental Security Income (SSI) (pages 172-174), and many nursing home patients after they have exhausted their own funds.

The majority of persons on Medicaid are children and nonelderly adults. The majority of Medicaid expenditures, however, are for the elderly, with most such money paying for nursing home care.

Strict federal guidelines have been enacted in recent years, which are intended to greatly restrict the ability of nursing home patients to transfer their assets to other family members and still qualify for Medicaid. To determine the specific eligibility requirements that exist in your state, contact your state or county Medical Assistance office.

10 *Miscellaneous*

Social Security Rules

Retirement

(1) **Credits Needed:** 40 for persons born after 1/1/29. For others, fewer years are needed.

(2) **Number of Years of Earnings Needed:** 35 for persons born after 1/1/29. For others, fewer years are needed.

Disability

(3) **Credits Needed:** Count the number of years **after** you became 21 **through** the year before disability occurs (or **through** the year you become age 61, if earlier). That's how many **credits** you need to be fully insured. To qualify for disability benefits, you must also meet another requirement — 20 credits during the 40 calendar quarters ending with the calendar quarter in which you become disabled. If you do not meet this requirement, then:

   (a) If you become disabled at ages 24-31 and do not meet the 20/40 requirement above, you need one credit for each two calendar quarters after the time you reached 21 and before the time you become disabled, but not less than six credits.

   (b) If you become disabled before age 24 and do not meet the 20/40 requirement above, you need six credits in the 12-quarter period ending with the quarter you become disabled.

(4) **Number of Years of Earnings Needed:** You subtract drop-out years from the number of credits you need to be fully insured for disability on the basis described in the first sentence of item 3. The number of drop-out years is:

Age Disability Occurs	Drop-out Years
Under age 27	0
27-31	1
32-36	2
37-41	3
42-46	4
47+	5

The remainder is the number of years of earnings you must use to figure your AIME. The result cannot be less than two years. However, persons disabled before age 37 may have additional child-care drop-out years (page 78).

Death

(5) **Credits Needed:** Count the number of years **after** you became 21 (do not count any year before 1951) **through** the year before death occurs (or **through** the year you become age 61, if earlier). The result cannot be less than six. That's how many credits you need to be fully insured so that your dependents are qualified for all survivor benefits.

(6) **Number of Years of Earnings Needed:** Subtract five from the number of credits you need to be fully insured for survivor benefits. The result cannot be less than two. That's how many years of earnings you use to figure your AIME.

Primary Insurance Amount (PIA) formula

(7) **For Persons Attaining Age 62** in one of the years shown below (or becoming disabled or dying in that year, before age 62), the PIA formula applied to the AIME is:

Age 62 in	PIA Benefit Formula		
	90% of	32% of	15% of
1999	**First $505**	**Next $2,538**	**Over $3,043**
1998	477	2,398	2,875
1997	455	2,286	2,741
1996	437	2,198	2,635
1995	426	2,141	2,567
1994	422	2,123	2,545
1993	401	2,019	2,420
1992	387	1,946	2,333
1991	370	1,860	2,230

To the resulting monthly benefit figure, apply cost-of-living adjustments (COLAs) for the year age 62 is attained and **all subsequent years, as follows:**

Year	COLA	Year	COLA
1991	3.7%	1995	2.6%
1992	3.0	1996	2.9
1993	2.6	1997	2.1
1994	2.8	1998	1.3

Note: These COLAs were effective for December and normally payable beginning in January.

The annual cost-of-living adjustment (COLA) for a particular year is determined by comparing price inflation for the third calendar quarter of that year with the same quarter of the previous year. Used for this purpose is the Consumer Price Index for Urban Wage Earners and Clerical Workers (CPI-W).

Maximum Family Benefit (MFB) formula

(8) For persons attaining age 62 in one of the years shown (or dying before age 62 in such year), the MFB formula applied to the PIA is:

	MFB Benefit Formula			
Age 62 in	**150% of**	**272% of**	**134% of**	**175% of**
1999	**First $645**	**Next $286**	**Next $283**	**Over $1,214**
1998	609	271	267	1,147
1997	581	258	255	1,094
1996	559	247	246	1,052
1995	544	241	239	1,024
1994	539	240	237	1,016
1993	513	227	226	966
1992	495	219	217	931
1991	473	209	208	890
1990	455	201	200	856

For disabled persons, the MFB is the smaller of (a) 150% of PIA, or (b) 85% of the AIME, but not less than the PIA. To the resulting monthly benefit figure, apply the appropriate cost-of-living adjustments for subsequent years.

Reduction factors for early retirement

If a benefit begins before the Full Retirement Age (FRA), it is reduced as follows:

Worker . . . . $5/9$ of 1% per month for the first 36 months, plus $5/12$ of 1% for each additional month

Spouse . . . . $25/36$ of 1% per month for the first 36 months, plus $5/12$ of 1% for each additional month

Surviving spouse . . . . $28\frac{1}{2}$% at age 60 (prorated for months between age 60 and the FRA)

Disabled surviving spouse
   at ages 50-59 . . . . $28\frac{1}{2}$%

Note: As the Full Retirement Age (FRA) rises, the factor for the early retirement benefit at age 62 will gradually decline, starting in 2000, from 80% of the Primary Insurance Amount (PIA) to 70% of the PIA. Similarly, a spouse's early retirement benefit at age 62 will gradually change from 75% to 65% of the amount available at the FRA. Beginning in 2000, reductions will also be larger that at present for surviving spouses first claiming benefits after age 60.

Benefit Eligibility Status for Remarried Spouses

Many persons reaching retirement age have been married more than once. The chart in this section describes what effect, if any, that remarriage has on eligibility for spouse or survivor benefits.

The chart shows the situation for a woman who was married twice — under all possible conditions as to current age, the age at remarriage, and whether or not the husbands involved are still living. **Although the chart relates to women, it is equally applicable to men;** however, few men receive husband's or widower's benefits because the benefit based on their own earnings record is usually larger.

Some of the annotations are marked "not applicable" (n/a). This is done when the basic eligibility requirements are not met rather than marital status being the relevant factor. Examples: (1) Wife's benefits are not payable before age 62 and (2) Widow's benefits are not payable if the husband is living.

In the case of a woman who had been married more than twice, the chart can be used, in turn, to determine the eligibility status on the basis of each husband's work record by considering the particular ex-husband as "First Husband" and the last husband (or ex-husband) as "Second Husband." For example, in the case of a woman age 68 who had been married three times, with the second remarriage occurring after age 60, and whose first and third husbands are deceased, she is eligible for widow's benefits on the earnings records of both the first and third husbands — according to the last line of the chart — and to divorced wife's benefits on the earnings record of the second husband (if the marriage lasted at least 10 years) — according to the next-to-last line of the chart. She, of course, receives only the largest of such three benefits.

Benefit Eligibility Status for Remarried Woman (Non-Disabled and Without Eligible Child) Under Various Conditions

Current Age of Woman	Age at Remarriage	Status of First Husband	Status of Second Husband	Wife's Benefit on		Widow's Benefit on	
				First Husband	Second Husband	First Husband	Second Husband
60-61	Under 60	*	Alive	n/a	n/a	No	n/a
60-61	Under 60	Alive	Deceased	n/a	n/a	n/a	Yes
60-61	Under 60	Deceased	Deceased	n/a	n/a	Yes	Yes
60-61	60+	Alive	Alive	n/a	n/a	n/a	n/a
60-61	60+	Alive	Deceased	n/a	n/a	n/a	Yes
60-61	60+	Deceased	Alive	n/a	n/a	Yes	n/a
60-61	60+	Deceased	Deceased	n/a	n/a	Yes	Yes
62+	Under 60	Alive	Alive	No	Yes	n/a	n/a
62+	Under 60	Alive	Deceased	Yes	n/a	n/a	Yes
62+	Under 60	Deceased	Alive	n/a	Yes	No	n/a
62+	Under 60	Deceased	Deceased	n/a	n/a	Yes	Yes
62+	60+	Alive	Alive	No	Yes	n/a	n/a
62+	60+	Alive	Deceased	Yes	n/a	n/a	Yes
62+	60+	Deceased	Alive	n/a	Yes	Yes	n/a
62+	60+	Deceased	Deceased	n/a	n/a	Yes	Yes

* Regardless of whether alive or deceased

Note: Second marriage assumed to terminate only by death. Second marriage assumed to have lasted at least one year. First marriage assumed to have lasted at least 10 years.

155

Garnishment

Social Security benefits are protected by law from assignment, levy, or garnishment. The only exceptions are: levies by the IRS for unpaid federal taxes, and garnishment orders issued by courts for the enforcement of legal obligations to provide child support or make alimony payments.

Members of the Armed Forces

Members of the armed forces of the U.S. have been covered by Social Security since 1957. **They pay taxes on their cash compensation.** Further, they receive additional earnings credits of $100 for each $300 of actual earnings, up to a maximum of $1,200 of additional credit per year. (These additional credits were $300 per quarter in 1957-77.) This reflects the value of the food, housing, and clothing that they receive. These additional credits are not always granted if military service is shorter than two years.

For service in 1951-1956, military personnel received free earnings credits of $160 per month. These credits are not always granted if a federal pension is payable for the same period of service.

Credits that are based on other than actual pay received do not always appear on the Social Security earnings record, but they are used when a benefit application is made, if the credits result in a larger benefit.

Living Outside the U.S.

If you are a Social Security beneficiary, and you live outside of the U.S. for 30 days or more, you must notify the Social Security Administration. This applies even if you have direct deposit of your benefit to a financial institution in the U.S.

The U.S. consists of the 50 states, District of Columbia, American Samoa, Guam, Northern Mariana Islands, Puerto Rico, and U.S. Virgin Islands.

People can usually continue to receive Social Security benefits while living outside the U.S. More restrictive rules apply to persons living outside the U.S. who are not U.S. citizens and are receiving benefits as a dependent or survivor. Social Security will make a determination in each case.

The annual earnings test is replaced with a foreign work test for beneficiaries who work outside the U.S. If you work outside of the U.S. in employment not subject to U.S. Social Security taxes, then work of more than 45 hours a month will cause your benefit to be withheld. There is no limitation once you reach age 70.

If you are neither a U.S. citizen nor a U.S. resident, then 25.5% of your benefit will usually be withheld for federal income tax. This withholding is sometimes reduced or eliminated according to terms of treaties with other countries.

Many foreign countries tax U.S. Social Security benefits. You should contact the embassy in Washington, D.C. of the country in which you plan to live for more information.

Medicare does not cover health services received outside of the U.S., except in very limited circumstances in Canada, and along the U.S. and Mexican border. If you are outside of the U.S. for a long time, you may not want to enroll in or continue Medicare Part B, because of the monthly premium required. However, if you do not enroll, or if you disenroll, there is a premium surcharge of 10 percent per year of nonenrollment if you reenroll later. In such cases, you could reenroll only during the first three months of the year, and coverage would not be effective until the following July (page 107).

International Social Security Agreements

Legislation in 1977 authorized the President to enter into bilateral totalization agreements with other nations for limited coordination of the Social Security program (but not Medicare) with corresponding programs of the other countries. The earnings records of persons who work in the countries with which agreements have been made will be combined for purposes of determining benefit eligibility. Currently, in such agreements, the combination of earnings records is done only for eligibility purposes. When eligibility is obtained **only** because of such totalization, the benefit amount is computed in a special manner.

Another feature of these agreements is that dual simultaneous coverage (and thus dual payment of payroll taxes) will be eliminated. In other words, a citizen of the United States employed in another country by a U.S. employer (and whose coverage under Social Security thus continues) will not be covered under the social insurance system of a nation with which an agreement had been made (as would otherwise have been the case). The same situation, of course, prevails for foreigners working in the United States for an employer of their own country.

Agreements with the following countries are now in effect: Austria, Belgium, Canada, Finland, France, Germany, Greece, Ireland, Italy, Luxembourg, Netherlands, Norway, Portugal, Spain, Sweden, Switzerland, and the United Kingdom. Agreements with other countries are in various stages of negotiation.

Railroad Retirement System

The Social Security program, as indicated previously, covers virtually all nongovernment employment in the United States except for railroad employees, who are covered by the Railroad Retirement system. This separate system is coordinated closely with Social Security, and its general structure is quite similar, although the retirement benefits are significantly higher, and the retirement conditions are somewhat more liberal.

It may be said that Railroad Retirement is a social insurance program, although it has certain characteristics of a large multi-employer, private pension plan. It is administered by the Railroad Retirement Board, with headquarters in Chicago, in conjunction with certain other benefit programs for railroad employees (namely, unemployment insurance and cash sickness benefits).

In order to receive Railroad Retirement benefits, the worker must have at least 10 years of railroad service. If such is not the case, the railroad wages are transferred to Social Security and are counted towards benefits in the usual manner. Railroad Retirement benefits consist of two parts — (1) what is essentially a Social Security benefit and (2) an amount proportionately related to the length of service and the average earnings in the highest 60 months of service.

The conditions for receipt of Railroad Retirement benefits are at least as favorable as under Social Security, and in some instances much more favorable. For example, individuals can retire at age 62 with 30 years of service without the usual reduction for early retirement. Also, disability annuities are available for occupational disability, rather than the strict standards required by Social Security. Further, widowed spouse's benefits are available at age 60, with the reduction for early retirement being only that applicable to retirement at age 62.

Railroad workers and their employers pay exactly the same taxes as do other workers for Social Security and the Hospital Insurance portion of Medicare. They are covered for Medicare just as are all other workers. In addition, in order to finance the more liberal cash benefits, railroad employers pay a tax of 16.1%, and railroad employees pay a tax of 4.9%. The maximum amount on which these taxes are paid is $53,700 in 1999 (which is automatically adjusted each year, in the same manner as is the Social Security maximum taxable amount). Employers also pay a tax that is used to finance supplemental annuities.

The Notch

The "Notch" is one of the most misunderstood and controversial Social Security issues in many years. This term refers to a special method of calculating Social Security benefits for people born in **1917-21,** the result of legislation enacted in 1977. Twenty-two years later, this issue is still being discussed. These "notch babies" believe that they are receiving less favorable benefit treatment than those born earlier and later. This, in fact, is true only as between persons born in 1917-21 who worked well beyond age 62 and those born **before** 1917 who also worked well beyond age 62.

In 1972, Congress changed the method for calculating Social Security benefits. The purpose of this change was to have inflation reflected in Social Security benefits. The 1972 law, however, did not work in the way intended because of dramatic changes in the relationship of wage and price inflation. The result was that Social Security benefits were over-indexed for inflation. Benefits soon escalated to levels much higher than Congress intended. This caused a severe strain on the financial stability of the Social Security system, and Congress soon recognized that corrective action was required.

In 1977, Congress corrected the method by which the effects of inflation are reflected in calculating Social Security benefits. The purpose was to bring benefits back to levels historically intended by Congress and avert a financial crisis for the Social Security system.

Congress faced a dilemma though on the issue of fairness. If retirement benefits were lowered only for those becoming eligible in the future, then these persons would feel unfairly disadvantaged. However, lowering benefits for those retirees already receiving benefits, or eligible to receive benefits, was considered even less fair. Congress decided to let older retirees, those born before 1917, keep their unintended windfall. People born after 1921 would have their benefits calculated under the new law.

But people born during 1917-1921, who were close to 60 when the law was passed, were given special treatment. For these so-called notch babies, the law provided two ways to calculate benefits, and beneficiaries would get whichever one was better. Benefits for the notch babies are sometime lower than for older people, because they don't get part of the accidental windfall. But benefits are sometimes better than for younger people.

Unfortunately, many of the notch babies are misinformed about the effect of the law and think they're being cheated. In fact, the opposite is true for many such recipients. The real problem: there's no good way to correct the mistake of letting benefits get too high under the 1972 law. If Congress took the windfall away from people who had already retired, it would seem unfair to people who had made financial plans based on a certain income expectation. On the other hand, if it extended the windfall to a further age group, people just under the age would complain that they deserve it too — exactly what the notch babies say.

Appealing Unfavorable Decisions

With the exception of the disability determinations, almost all Social Security claims are decided on clear-cut issues. The overwhelming majority of appeals are filed on disability claims. A claimant has 60 days from receipt of a written notice to file an appeal.

The appeal process proceeds as follows:

(1) **Reconsideration:** A reconsideration entails a complete re-examination of the claim by a different decision-maker.

(2) **Hearing:** A hearing is conducted by an administrative law judge. A claimant can appear in person at the hearing. It is at this stage that many claimants decide to be represented by an attorney.

(3) **Appeals Council Review:** Appeals Council Review involves a technical review of the decision of the administrative law judge for conformity with applicable laws and regulations.

(4) **U.S. District Court:** This is the first step of the regular federal judicial process in which a dissatisfied applicant brings suit against the government.

History of Social Security

Many factors contributed to passage of the Social Security Act of 1935. As the U.S. changed rapidly from an agricultural to an industrial economy, individuals became less self-sufficient. The Great Depression of the early 1930s caused many political leaders to believe that the time had come to enact federal legislation to relieve social problems that existed. Most other industrial nations had passed comprehensive social insurance laws many years earlier.

Payroll taxes began January 1, 1937. The rate for both employees and employers was 1% on earnings up to $3,000 per year, or a maximum tax each of $30. This tax level continued through 1949, and there were few benefit changes during this period after the very significant amendments in 1939 (see page 164). The tax increases that have taken place since then are shown on page 16; benefit increases have generally kept pace with inflation.

Congress has made amendments to Social Security many times in its long history. Some of the most significant changes follow.

1939   Benefits for dependents and survivors added to the law (page 12);

1950   Coverage extended to 10 million additional persons, primarily, nonfarm self-employed (except professionals); farm and domestic workers; U.S. citizens employed abroad by U.S. employers; federal employees not under a retirement system; employees of charitable, educational, and religious nonprofit organizations (on elective basis); and employees of state and local governments (on elective basis);

1954   Coverage extended to the farm self-employed and professionals (except doctors, dentists, and lawyers);

1956   Benefits established for disabled workers, ages 50 to 64, coverage extended to military personnel, dentists, and lawyers;

1960   Disability provisions extended to workers of all ages (pages 73-83);

1965   Medicare hospital insurance (Part A) and medical insurance (Part B) enacted (pages 101-125); coverage extended to doctors;

1972   Several types of annual automatic adjustments established. Effective each January 1, maximum taxable earnings base and the earnings limitation (retirement test) changed in accordance with pay levels. Effective each June, benefits changed, based on cost-of-living increases (page 151);

1977   Taxes increased; method of calculating benefits changed;

1980   Disability benefits for young workers and maximum family benefits in the event of disability both reduced;

1981   Minimum benefit of $122 a month eliminated; benefits for college students eliminated gradually during 1982-85;

1982 Age at which the earnings limitation no longer applies reduced from age 72 to age 70; employer-sponsored healthcare plans for employees ages 65 through 69, and their spouses, became primary payer, and Medicare the secondary payer; Medicare Part B premium established at 25% of the program cost, instead of tying changes in it to the COLA for cash benefits;

1983 Coverage extended to newly hired federal employees and on a compulsory basis to all employees of nonprofit organizations; COLA deferred for six months — to be paid each January, starting in 1984; larger increases for delayed retirement provided, beginning for persons reaching age 65 in 1990 and after (page 49); age at which full retirement benefits are paid gradually increased from 65 to 67, beginning in 2003 and reaching 67 in 2027 (page 44); retirement earnings test for persons reaching the Full Retirement Age liberalized, beginning in 1990 (page 54); scheduled Social Security tax rate increases accelerated; up to one-half of Social Security benefits made subject to federal income taxes for persons with high income from other sources (page 24); divorced spouses permitted to draw benefits after age 62 if ex-spouse is eligible for benefits (whether or not claimed); deceased worker's earnings to be indexed (adjusted for wage inflation) for years after death in computing deferred survivor benefits;

1986 Removal of age-70 ceiling for period when employer-sponsored healthcare plan is primary to Medicare; Medicare made secondary payer for disabled employees covered by an employer-sponsored healthcare plan as a current employee, providing employer has 100 employees or more (applies to family members, as well) (page 123);

1988 Medicare Catastrophic Coverage Act enacted, expanding benefits significantly and increasing costs to beneficiaries (effective for 1989 only, because the law was repealed in late 1989);

1990 Coverage extended to state and local government employees not covered by a retirement plan of their employer; taxable earnings base for 1.45% Medicare tax increased to $125,000 for 1991 (compared to $53,400 for the 6.2% Social Security tax) (page 14); Medicare Part B deductible increased from $75 to $100; physicians limited as to what they can charge Medicare patients, decreasing over three years to 115% of Medicare's allowable charges after 1992 (page 120);

1993 For 1994 and later years, taxes on Social Security benefits were increased, making up to 85% subject to federal income taxes for high-income beneficiaries; also, the earnings ceiling was removed for the 1.45% Medicare tax.

1996 Disability benefits are not payable to persons disabled solely due to alcoholism or drug addiction.

1997 Medicare+Choice enacted (page 138).

With the exception of railroad workers and some federal, state, and local government employees, virtually all workers are now covered by Social Security. Except for the fact that a portion of Medicare Part B expenses are paid from general revenues, Social Security and Medicare have not received any federal general revenues for permanent long-range features of law, but only money collected through payroll taxes, plus interest on the reserves, plus the income taxes on benefits. Such income, to the extent not needed for current benefit payments, is invested exclusively in government bonds.

The Future of Social Security

Social Security is currently quite healthy, but it faces serious long-term problems. The important 1983 amendments (see page 165), which were intended to restore financial health to the program for 75 years, have at least succeeded in the short-term. Since then, Social Security revenues have significantly outpaced expenditures. Annual payroll tax revenues are projected, according to the intermediate (most likely to occur) projections in the 1998 Trustees Report, to continue to exceed benefit payments until 2012. However, until 2021, tax revenues plus interest income on the trust-fund investments will exceed outgo each year. From 2021 until 2032, a combination of payroll taxes, trust fund interest, and use of the principal of the trust funds would enable the system to meet its obligations on time. However, beginning in 2032 the system would not be able to meet its obligations on time. This is a serious problem, but it is not an immediate crisis, nor does it need to be a crisis at all. The sooner, however, that measures are taken to address these projected long-range cash-flow problems, the less drastic such measures will need to be. Adjustments that are scheduled well in advance, and implemented on a gradual or incremental basis, can make a big difference.

The projected long-term problems for Social Security are of special concern to young and middle-aged people. Many are convinced that Social Security will either not be there for them when they reach retirement age, or at best, that it will only provide a much lower level of retirement-income protection than it traditionally has.

This decline in confidence can be attributed to a number of different factors including:

■ Frequent reports in the media that Social Security will eventually go bankrupt;

■ The assumed unsustainability of an income-transfer program that faces a decreasing ratio of workers to beneficiaries when the generation of baby boomers retires;

- Skepticism about whether the assets held by the Social Security trust funds are of real value or are just worthless government IOUs;

- Concerns about federal budget deficits and the national debt, and how so-called "entitlement programs" contribute to these problems; and

- A widespread lack of confidence in government programs.

A number of proposals are being made to address the long-range problems of Social Security. One such proposal is to lower future COLAs. Proponents argue that the current formula overstates inflation for retirees and that small adjustments can result in tremendous long-term savings for the system. Critics argue that inflation may actually be **understated** for retirees when full consideration is given to medical expenses. They also point out that COLAs are not really benefit increases, but rather that they merely maintain the purchasing power of current benefits.

There are some groups that advocate major reforms of the current system. Some argue that the trust fund reserves should be invested in the stock market rather than in special-issue Treasury obligations. They point out that the stock market has historically provided a significantly greater real rate of return. Critics of this approach point out that a conservative investment with a predictable return devoid of large fluctuations is more suitable for a national social insurance program. They also point out that not using trust fund assets to assist in financing current government borrowing will mean that the government would have to borrow more from the private sector to make up the difference. Further, they are concerned that the government, in having control of a large portion of the stock market, could have too much power in the private sector.

Another proposal receiving much attention calls for means-testing (actually income-testing) Social Security benefits. Advocates note that not only do Social Security benefits go to low- and middle-income persons, but also affluent persons receive benefits. Some characterize this as welfare for the rich. They question how we can afford to pay entitlements to the rich when we have a large national debt and a Social Security system facing insolvency. Critics of means-testing point out that Social Security is a self-funded program. Denying benefits to those persons who have paid the most into the system would be unfair and would undermine important public support for the program. Such persons already receive a smaller rate of return for their Social Security taxes than low-income persons. Excluding high-income persons would also make Social Security a welfare program and cause some stigmatization of those who receive benefits. They also point out that the means-testing of Social Security would act as a disincentive for individual savings and employer-sponsored retirement plans.

Others call for even more fundamental change. Proposals range from partial to full privatization of the system. Supporters of privatization point out that this would increase individual responsibility for retirement planning, that individuals would be able to achieve greater investment returns, and that it would cause a much needed improvement in the national savings rate. Critics argue that a privatized system would undermine the important social adequacy component of the system under which a basic floor of protection is provided for all participants through a broad pooling of risk. They also point out that proponents of privatization often overlook the important disability and survivor insurance components of the present system. Also, not everyone will be fortunate enough to realize substantial investment returns. It is also pointed out that any such major overhaul of the system would entail large transition costs which would have to be borne by the general treasury and also ongoing high administrative expenses (especially for the accounts for persons with low earnings).

There are others who favor the basic approach of the present system, which balances the components of social adequacy and individual equity (generally providing larger benefits to those who have paid more into the system). They maintain that long-range solvency for the system can be achieved through moderate adjustments. They generally advocate some combination of tax increases and benefit reductions.

These traditionalists maintain that necessary increases in the payroll tax rate or in the maximum taxable earnings base can be implemented in small increments and scheduled decades in advance. They further maintain that such tax increases should be far more than compensated for by the very likely greater increases in the productivity of the overall economy. They also advocate removing the special income tax treatment for Social Security benefits and taxing them the same way as any other contributory pension and continuing to direct such revenues back to the Social Security trust funds. Critics argue that taxes are already too high and that any increase in taxes, even ones scheduled many years in advance, are not politically feasible. In addition, traditionalist advocate extending mandatory coverage to all new state and local government employees (only about three-quarters of such employees are now covered).

On the benefit side of the equation, there are proposals to further gradually increase the age at which full retirement benefits are payable and/or accelerate increases already scheduled. This would not only save the system money, but it would also recognize the increasing life expectancy of retirees. There could be similar changes regarding when benefits are first payable for early retirement and the amount of the actuarial reduction for taking them early. In addition, certain technical changes in the benefit calculation formula could be implemented that would result in a slight decrease in benefit amounts. Critics argue that this will just further exacerbate the individual equity component of Social Security by increasing the length of time that it takes persons to get their money's worth from the program.

These are some of the proposals currently receiving much attention. Different groups and individuals advocate various versions and combinations of these and other proposals.

The debate on the future of Social Security is heating up. Social Security should continue to be financially strong for about 20 years and perhaps longer, but the long-range forecast is not so rosy. In addition to having long-range financial problems, the Social Security system must face these challenges in a political environment that increasingly doubts the effectiveness of government programs, and is reexamining the proper role of government.

11 *Supplemental Security Income*

Supplemental Security Income (SSI), is a federal assistance program for aged (65 or older), blind, and disabled persons with little or no income and resources. In some cases, such persons who are not citizens, but who are lawful residents, may also qualify.

SSI is administered by the Social Security Administration; however, it is a separate program from Social Security. SSI is financed by the general revenues of the government. The Social Security trust funds are not used for SSI. The Social Security Administration is reimbursed from the General Treasury for the expenses which it incurs for administering SSI.

The maximum federal SSI payment for an eligible individual in 1999 is $500 per month. It is $751 per month for an eligible couple. The basic SSI payment is reduced by one-third if an eligible person is living in another person's household and receiving support and maintenance in-kind from that person. The payment rate may be less if a person has other income. Many of the states supplement the federal payment. Amounts of state supplements vary. Most SSI recipients qualify for Medicaid, and many qualify for food stamps as well. Eligibility requirements for these programs can vary from state to state.

When establishing initial entitlement for SSI disability payments for adults, the same definition of disability is used as in the Social Security disability program. Disabled means that you are so severely impaired, physically or mentally that you cannot perform any substantial gainful work. The impairment must be expected to last at least 12 months or result in earlier death. A special, broader definition of disability is used for children. There is no five month waiting period for SSI disability payments as there is for Social Security disability benefits.

Not all income and resources are counted when determining eligibility and the payment amount. Your home, car, ordinary household items, burial plot, and $1,500 face value of life insurance are generally not counted. An individual is allowed $2,000 in savings or other countable assets. A couple is allowed $3,000. There is a $20 per month income exclusion. In addition, $65 per month of **earned** income, plus one-half of the remainder of **earned** income is excluded when determining countable income. This earned income exclusion is intended to encourage those who are able to work to do so. A portion of the income and resources of ineligible spouses and parents who live in the same household is considered when determining the countable income of an SSI applicant or recipient.

An aged, blind, or disabled person who receives a small Social Security benefit may also qualify for SSI.

Example: Ms. Adams is 65 and receives a gross Social Security benefit (before deduction for the Medicare Part B premium) of $400. She has no other income and meets all other requirements for SSI eligibility. She can receive $120 in SSI payments.

$400.00	Social Security benefit (gross)
− 20.00	Income exclusion
$380.00	Countable income
$500.00	Maximum SSI payment rate
− 380.00	Countable income
$120.00	SSI payment

In this example, her gross monthly income is $520 ($400.00 Social Security and $120.00 SSI). Her net monthly income is $474.50 after she has her Part B premium of $45.50 deducted from her Social Security benefit.

In addition, Ms. Adams should contact her state or local medical assistance office to see if she qualifies for Medicaid, or if she is eligible to be a Qualified Medicare Beneficiary or a Specified Low-Income Medicare Beneficiary so that the state will pay her Part B monthly premium for her. If she qualifies, then her net monthly income will increase by $45.50 for a total of $520.

If you know someone who might qualify for SSI, you should encourage them to contact the Social Security Administration right away and apply for benefits. There is no provision to pay any retroactive SSI before the effective filing date.

SSI payments are normally issued on the first day of the month, representing payment for that month. If the first is on a Saturday, Sunday, or holiday, then payment is made on the preceding business day.

You should do several things to make sure you get all the benefits to which you are entitled. Some of these things should be done now. Others should be done later.

Remember this: Social Security will not start your benefits until you file an application. Start with a telephone call to the Social Security Administration's national toll-free number: **800-772-1213.** Most applications can be taken by phone.

If you are late in filing an application, you may not be paid all of the benefits which you could have received.

When To Do It	What To Do
Now	■ Everyone (even children) should have a Social Security number and a card showing that number. It's needed when you buy a government bond, open a savings account, and when you get a job. The law requires a child to have a Social Security number to be claimed as a dependent on an income tax return. ■ Complete and mail Form SSA-7004 attached in this book. The form is labeled "Request for Earnings and Benefit Estimate Statement." Sign the form before mailing it.

When you receive your Earnings and Benefit Estimate Statement

■ As soon as you receive the Statement, check the earnings information for errors. If you find an error, call Social Security.

When you file your federal income tax return

■ If you have had more than one job and earned more than the maximum for Social Security for that year, you probably have paid excess taxes. You should claim a credit for these excess taxes when you file your federal income tax return. Your W-2 forms show how much you paid. Look at the boxes labeled "Social Security tax withheld."

Before you file for benefits

■ Because you do not know when disability or death claims might have to be filed, why not get papers ready now? Make sure you have a certified copy of your birth certificate. Social Security cannot use ordinary photocopies. If you are filing for benefits based on your spouse's or former spouse's earnings record, you may need to present a certified copy of your marriage certificate. If you apply for benefits as a divorced spouse, you will also need your divorce decree.

Three months or more before you start benefits

■ File an application. Processing an application takes time. Always start the process at least three months before the date you want retirement benefits to begin. To be safe, do so in the January before you intend to retire, but not earlier than four months before you turn 62. Disability or survivor benefits should be filed for as soon as possible after disability or death occurs. Any application can be started by calling the Social Security Administration's national toll-free number **800-772-1213.**

If you think a decision by Social Security is wrong

■ If you believe that a decision by Social Security is wrong, you can appeal within 60 days. Start by calling Social Security. They will tell you how to have your case reviewed. Several levels of appeal are possible within the Social Security Administration. After that, you can appeal to the federal courts, but you will need a lawyer.

Any time

■ If you think you may be eligible for benefits, file an application. **Don't just ask** if you are eligible. An informal question is never given the attention that an application receives. If an application is incorrectly denied, its filing date will be used when your benefits start.

After you retire

■ After you start receiving benefits, if your earnings exceed the earnings limitation (pages 54-58), call Social Security and report this information to them. Having benefits withheld is less painful than having to pay back benefits that should not have been paid to you. And if benefits are paid incorrectly, you **will** have to pay them back.

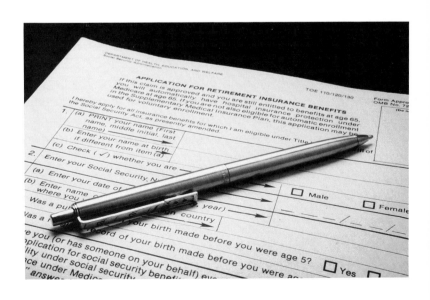

When you reach age 70	■ The earnings limitation does not apply beginning with the month when you reach age 70. You can then earn any amount without losing any benefits.
If disabled	■ File your application promptly so that it can be processed during the waiting period. Cooperate with any instructions regarding rehabilitation services. If you have a good reason not to do what is requested, call Social Security and discuss it with them. All earnings from work must be reported if you are receiving disability benefits.
Mother or father	■ If you are receiving benefits because you have a child in your care, and the child leaves your care, report it at once. Payments made improperly **will** have to be repaid.
If you lose your card	■ Call Social Security and give them all the information they request. They will arrange for you to receive a replacement card with the same number. **Do not apply for a new number.** A record of all your earnings is filed under this number. You should be sure that you receive credit for all your work.

When you are close to retirement age	■ If you can choose the time to retire, look carefully at the Earnings Limitation. You may be able to start your benefits effective January 1 and keep on working until you have earned the annual limit (page 54) before actually stopping work. In this case, you would lose no benefits at all.
If you travel outside the U.S.	■ Remember that Medicare does not pay for hospital or other medical expenses outside the U.S. (exceptions are qualified Canadian and Mexican facilities if they are nearest to your home, or if for emergency care while traveling to or from Alaska through Canada). If you plan to travel abroad, consider obtaining additional insurance.
If you become eligible for a second benefit	■ Sometimes you can become eligible for a benefit on someone else's work record even though you are already receiving a benefit on your own record. Call Social Security and tell them all the facts. Tell them you want to file an application. When they know about both benefits, they will figure both, and you will get the larger one. If they do not know about one benefit because you do not apply, they cannot check to see if you should be receiving more.

Remember

■ Social Security will not ordinarily look for you to pay you a benefit. They will not take any action until you apply. Then they will process your application carefully and with reasonable speed, considering that 45 million people now receive Social Security benefits each month.

You have to apply for your benefit.

13 *Frequently Asked Questions*

Social Security

Q. Will I receive Social Security benefits on my own Social Security work record or on my spouse's? Can I get both?

A. If you are eligible for more than one type of benefit at the same time, the most you can receive is the equivalent of the higher benefit. When you apply for benefits, Social Security will automatically calculate all possible benefits for which you are eligible. If you are eligible for both a retirement benefit and a spouse's benefit, then you will receive the retirement benefit and the excess, **if any,** by which the spouse's benefit exceeds the retirement benefit. If you are eligible for both a retirement benefit and a surviving spouse's benefit, then again the most you can receive is the equivalent of the higher benefit. In this situation, however, you can receive a reduced benefit on one Social Security record and then switch to an unreduced benefit, if higher, on the other Social Security record at or near your Full Retirement Age (currently 65). Social Security will calculate all possible options and advise you accordingly.

Q. If I retire before I am old enough for Social Security, what effect will this have on the amount of my future Social Security benefit?

A. Persons who work continually from their early twenties and retire in their mid to late fifties will find that early retirement has only a minimal effect on the average earnings used to compute their Social Security benefit. Social Security retirement benefits are determined by career average earnings subject to the Social Security tax.

The 35 highest years of earnings are considered for people born after 1928. If you work fewer than 35 years, then some years of zero earnings will be averaged in. If you work more than 35 years, then the low years of earnings in excess of 35 will be dropped from consideration. Earnings in years prior to age 60 are indexed to reflect wage inflation. Actual earnings are used after age 59.

Q. I have earned the maximum required 40 credits. Does this mean that I get the maximum Social Security retirement benefit?

A. No. Having 40 credits means that you are insured for a Social Security retirement benefit. The amount of your benefit is determined by your career average earnings covered by Social Security, and the age at which you begin receiving benefits.

Q. My ex-husband and I were divorced several years ago after more than 10 years of marriage. We are both age 62. He worked in a much higher paying job than I did. Can I receive Social Security divorced spouse's benefits on his work record?

A. Yes, assuming that you are not currently remarried, and that you are not entitled to a higher benefit on any other Social Security work record, including your own. It does not matter if he is remarried. Nor is it necessary for him to have started receiving his own benefits yet, as long as he is eligible for benefits. If you were still married to him, you could not start spouse's benefits on his work record until he started his own.

Q. I am the ex-husband in the previous question. I am remarried. Does the Social Security spouse benefit paid to my ex-wife in any way reduce the amount of benefits payable to me or my current wife?

A. No.

Q. I do not have enough credits to qualify for Social Security benefits. Can I voluntarily pay Social Security taxes to earn additional credits?

A. No. You can only earn Social Security credits by working in covered employment or self-employment. This is consistent with the overall purpose of the program, which is to help replace the earnings which are lost due to retirement, disability, or death.

Q. If I start collecting Social Security retirement benefits when I turn 62, when do I get my first payment?

A. Entitlement to retirement or aged spouse benefits cannot begin until the first full month that you are age 62. If your birthday is on the first or second day of the month, then you are considered to be 62 throughout the month of your birthday. If your birthday is after the second of the month, then the following month is the first full month that you are 62. Your first payment is not normally due until the month following your month of entitlement. Social Security will notify you as to which day of the month your benefit payment will normally be made.

Example 1: 62nd birthday on April 1 or 2. Your first month of entitlement is April and your first benefit is normally paid in May.

Example 2: 62nd birthday on April 3. Your first month of entitlement is May and your first benefit is normally paid in June.

Q. My father died on the last day of January. Can we keep the Social Security benefit that arrived for him in February?

A. No. The payment received in February is actually the benefit for January. Benefits are not due for the month of death. If he had died on February 1, then he would have lived throughout the month of January and the benefit could be reissued to an eligible survivor, or if none, then to the estate.

Q. I am 62, retired, financially well off, and don't need Social Security retirement benefits to meet my current expenses. Should I go ahead and elect to receive reduced benefits beginning at age 62 or should I wait until I'm 65 and receive the full benefit amount?

A. There is no simple answer to this question. Retirees have to make their own informed decisions. Retirement benefits are permanently reduced $\frac{5}{9}$ of 1% for each month of entitlement to benefits prior to age 65. This currently equals a 20% reduction at age 62. (See page 44 for scheduled increases in the full retirement age for people born after 1937.) Persons who choose to start their benefits before age 65 receive less per month than they would receive by waiting until 65, but they will of course, receive benefits for a longer period of time. The initial advantage of receiving reduced benefits will keep a person ahead, in terms of total lifetime benefits received, for 15 years. The initial advantage lasts until age 77 for a person who starts benefits at age 62, and it lasts until age 80 for a person who starts benefits at age 64 years and 11 months. If the unneeded benefits are saved or invested, then any accumulated interest or investment gain will increase the initial advantage. If income taxes are due on benefits received, then this will also have an effect.

And finally, one's health condition and the resulting life expectancy will be a major factor of consideration. The current life expectancy for a person who is 65 is about 15½ years for a man and 19 years for a woman. (See pages 50-53 for a detailed discussion.)

Q. Is the money in the Social Security trust funds used for other government programs besides Social Security?

A. Indirectly, yes.

By law, the revenues from Social Security taxes can only be used to pay for Social Security benefits and the administrative expenses of the program, which average less than 1% of benefits. Any excess must be invested in U.S. government securities. Both the principal and interest on these securities is guaranteed by the full faith and credit of the United States. When the Social Security trust funds buy these U.S. government securities, they are loaning the money to the government and thus helping to finance the national debt in the same manner as anyone else who buys a treasury bill or bond. The government in turn uses this borrowed money to pay the costs for many other government programs.

This is similar in principle to the situation of a person who deposits money into a savings account. The financial institution agrees to repay the principal plus interest to the depositor. The financial institution takes that money and lends it to someone else, who may use that money to buy a home or a car. In that sense, the person who deposited money into a savings account is indirectly financing someone else's purchase of a home or car.

Q. I was seriously injured in an accident and I am now disabled and unable to return to work. I have heard that there is a five or six month waiting period for Social Security disability. I have also heard that you have to be disabled a year to qualify for disability. This is all very confusing. When should I apply to the Social Security Administration for disability benefits?

A. You should apply now!

One of the requirements to qualify for disability benefits is that the disability must be expected to last at least 12 months or result in earlier death. This doesn't mean that the disability has actually lasted for 12 months, but rather that it is expected to last at least 12 months.

There is a waiting period of five full calendar months after the onset of disability before entitlement to benefits can begin. In effect, this often means as many as six or seven months before benefits are payable. For example, if you became disabled on January 2, then the five full months of your waiting period would be February through June. In this example, July would be the first month of entitlement and the benefit for July would not be due until August.

Also, the disability claim process can be very lengthy. It usually takes the Social Security Administration at least three months to process a disability claim. Furthermore, a large percentage of claims are only approved upon appeal after originally being denied. Thus, it is very important to apply as soon as possible.

Q. I am age 66 and receive Social Security surviving spouse benefits. If I remarry, will I lose my benefits?

A. No. Remarriage does not terminate surviving spouse benefits to widows or widowers age 60 and older, or disabled widows and widowers age 50 and older. Remarriage before attaining the minimum age to qualify for benefits does preclude entitlement to surviving spouse benefits as long as the subsequent marriage continues. If the subsequent marriage should end in death or divorce, then entitlement to benefits on the prior spouse's work record is permitted. (See pages 154-155 for a detailed discussion.)

Young widows and widowers who are entitled to benefits because they care for a child lose their benefits if they remarry. However, the child's benefits are unaffected by the remarriage of the parent.

Q. Why does the Social Security annual earnings test penalize the person who works, but not the person who has substantial investment income? This seems very unfair.

A. Unlike welfare, Social Security is not a means tested program. Social Security retirement benefits are intended to be insurance for loss of income due to retirement, not as insurance for attaining age 65.

Social Security is not designed to be a person's only source of retirement income. Rather, it is intended to provide a base of income to which the retired person can add other sources of retirement income such as employer-sponsored pensions and personal investments. By not considering investment income for purposes of the earnings test, individual savings is encouraged.

Q. My wife and I both receive Social Security benefits. My benefit is higher. If I die first, how much will her widow's benefit be?

A. If she is at least 65 when you die, then her total benefit will be what your benefit was, or in some cases slightly higher (page 91). It can be less if she is younger than 65 when you die (page 90).

Q. I retired last year at age 68 and started receiving my Social Security benefits. My wife, who is not insured for benefits on her own work record, became entitled to a spouse's benefit on my work record when she was 66. Why is her benefit less than one-half of mine? Both of us waited until after age 65 to start our Social Security. I thought her benefit was supposed to be one-half of mine.

A. Your benefit is increased because you earned Delayed Retirement Credits. You earned a DRC for each month that you did not receive a benefit after attaining age 65. These DRC's are applied only to your benefit, not to your wife's. If you die first, however, these DRC's will be used to increase the amount of the survivor benefit payable to your wife. (See page 49 for the various DRC rates based on different years of birth.)

Q. My wife and I have both worked in high-paying jobs. We will each be eligible for Social Security retirement benefits based on our own work records. Will our combined benefits be limited by a family maximum?

A. No. The family maximum rule can only apply when multiple benefits are payable on the same Social Security work record.

Medicare

Q. My wife and I will visit Europe this summer. Will Medicare cover us over there if we require emergency medical treatment?

A. No. Medicare does not cover medical treatment received outside of the United States except in qualified Canadian and Mexican facilities if they are nearest to your home, or for emergency care in Canada while traveling between Alaska and the "lower 48" states. If you have other health insurance, you should check to see if that policy provides foreign travel protection.

Q. Are Medicare and Medicaid the same thing?

A. No. Medicare is a federal program of health insurance for eligible persons age 65 and older, Social Security disability beneficiaries who have been entitled to monthly benefits for two years, and eligible persons with kidney failure. Financial status is not a factor of eligibility. You apply with the Social Security Administration for entitlement to Medicare.

Medicaid is a joint federal/state program of medical assistance for eligible persons with low income and resources. Applications for Medicaid are filed with the state or local Medicaid office or public assistance office.

Q. I will soon be 65. I am already retired, and I receive Social Security benefits. I have very good health insurance protection from my former employer. Do I need to enroll in Part B of Medicare and pay the monthly premium?

A. Generally yes, but not always. If the only employer sponsored health insurance you have is from the employer that you have retired from, then yes, you generally do need Part B. Your retiree health insurance will ordinarily revert to a Medicare supplement when you attain age 65.

However, if your spouse still works for an employer with 20 or more employees, and you have health insurance coverage under your spouse's employer sponsored health insurance plan, then the law requires that plan to remain as your primary health insurance. In this situation, you probably would not need to enroll in Part B until your spouse retires. You would, however, want to determine if there are any gaps in that coverage which Part B could fill and whether the additional benefit coverage is worth the Part B premium cost.

Q. My parents are over 65 and have never lived in the U.S. They are considering moving to the U.S. to be closer to me. Even though they are not eligible for monthly Social Security benefits, can they enroll in Medicare?

A. No, at least not right away. They will, however, be eligible to enroll in Medicare on a premium-payment basis either if they become U.S. citizens, or if they are lawfully admitted for permanent residence and have resided in the U.S. continuously for five years. They can enroll either for Parts A and B, or for Part B only. They cannot just take Part A.

The standard monthly premium rates in 1999 are $309 for premium Part A and $45.50 for Part B.

Q. What is SSI?

A. SSI stands for Supplemental Security Income. SSI is a federal program of financial assistance to the aged (age 65 or older), blind, and disabled who have little or no income and resources. Even though SSI is administered by the Social Security Administration, it is a different program than Social Security, and it is funded from general revenues, not from Social Security taxes (pages 172-174).

Q. I was born in 1938, and my Full Retirement Age for Social Security retirement benefits is 66 years and 2 months (see page 44). Will I have to wait until then to be eligible for Medicare?

A. No. You will be eligible for Medicare on the first day of the month that you attain age 65. The eligibility age for Medicare is not scheduled to increase.

Q. Are Medicare Part A (Hospital Insurance) and Part B (Medical Insurance) applicable to Medicare+Choice plans?

A. Yes. Parts A and B are applicable to both the Original Medicare Plan and Medicare+Choice plans. You must be enrolled in Parts A and B and pay the Part B monthly premium to be eligible to enroll in a Medicare+Choice plan (see page 138).

William M. Mercer, Incorporated, is the world's leading employee benefits and compensation consulting firm. We have offices in 41 U.S. cities. Worldwide, the Mercer organization has about 8,600 employees and offices in 106 cities in 27 countries. As we have expanded geographically, we have also increased services to meet clients' needs.

Other Social Security and Medicare information services include:

- 48-page Social Security booklet;
- 32-page Social Security booklet;
- 32-page Medicare booklet;
- quarterly newsletter;
- 48-page Professional's Reference;
- consulting services;
- retirement video;
- "giveaway" brochures and booklets for life insurance companies, banks and financial service companies.

Index